Musicians' Migratory Patterns

The Adriatic Coasts

**Edited by
Franco Sciannameo**

Routledge
Taylor & Francis Group

LONDON AND NEW YORK

First published 2018 by Routledge

2 Park Square, Milton Park, Abingdon, Oxfordshire OX14 4RN

52 Vanderbilt Avenue, New York, NY 10017

Routledge is an imprint of the Taylor & Francis Group, an informa business

First issued in paperback 2020

Copyright© 2018 Taylor & Francis

Library of Congress Cataloging-in-Publication Data
Names: Sciannameo, Franco, editor.
Title: Musicians' migratory patterns : the Adriatic coasts /
    edited by Franco Sciannameo.
Description: New York : Routledge, 2018. | Includes index. |
    Description based on print version record and CIP data provided
    by publisher; resource not viewed.
Identifiers: LCCN 2017048327 (print) | LCCN 2017052919 (ebook) |
    ISBN 9780203702024 | ISBN 9781138572508 (hardback)
Subjects: LCSH: Music—Adriatic Coast (Balkan Peninsula)—History
    and criticism. | Music—Italy—Adriatic Coast—History and criticism.
Classification: LCC ML250 (ebook) | LCC ML250 .M94 2018 (print) |
    DDC 780.9182/24—dc23
LC record available at https://lccn.loc.gov/2017048327

ISBN: 978-1-138-57250-8 (hbk)
ISBN: 978-0-367-60722-7 (pbk)

Typeset in Times New Roman
by Apex CoVantage, LLC

Musicians' Migratory Patterns

Musicians' Migratory Patterns: The Adriatic Coasts contains essays dedicated to the movement of musicians along and across the coasts of the Adriatic Sea. In the course of this book, the musicians become narrators of their own stories, seen through the lenses of wanderlust, opportunity, exile, and refuge. Essayists in this collection are scholars from Croatia, Italy, and Greece. They are internationally known for their passionate advocacy of musicians' migratory rights and for their fidelity to the lesson imparted by the history of immigration in the broadest of terms.

Spanning the Venetian Republic's domination, the demise of the Ottoman Empire, the European nationalistic movements of mid-nineteenth century, the shocking outcomes of World War I, and the dramatic shifts of frontiers that continue to occur in our time, the chapters of this book guide the reader on a voyage through the Adriatic Sea from the Gulf of Venice to Albania, the island of Corfu, and other Ionian outposts.

Franco Sciannameo is College Distinguished Teaching Professor of Musicology in the College of Fine Arts at Carnegie Mellon University. He is Visiting Professor of Applied Musicology in the Faculty of Arts, Humanities, and Cultures at the University of Leeds, UK.

In memory of Predrag Matvejević
(1932–2017)

Contents

Figures

Tables

Series Foreword

Created in 2009, *Cultural Expressions in Music* began as a series of monographs that sought to promote and share the diversity of perspectives, cultures, experiences, philosophies, and contributions of The College Music Society's membership and the music community at large. This series has now entered a new phase. The volumes published under this rubric follow the tenets of geo-musicology, an interdisciplinary outreach of recent coinage, which integrates musical expression, geo-political thinking, and migratory movement of musicians, musical genres, styles, repertoire, and practices. Forthcoming monographs and edited collections will urge readers worldwide to reflect, musically and culturally, upon one of the most pressing issues of our time: immigration.

Franco Sciannameo
Series Editor

Preface

This book, *Musicians' Migratory Patterns: The Adriatic Coasts*, heralds the new CMS Cultural Expressions series of monographs, whose goal is to provide informed and urgent messages about one of the most pressing issues of our time: immigration.

It is not a guide book about the coastal Adriatic people and their musical expressions but rather a collection of scholarly reflections on the disparate predicaments that led legions of musicians to wander along and across the Adriatic Sea in search of work opportunities, adventures, exile, and desperate refuge. Although these migratory patterns have remained unchanged over the centuries, the beacons of light that once consoled the migrants' anguish and guided them to safety are no longer beaming. The Adriatic lighthouses have become tourist attractions that resemble quixotic windmills unwilling to tell the stories they witnessed. This book of reflections wishes to bring the lighthouses' spirit back and shed new light upon their memories.[1]

Our hypothetical voyage among the Adriatic lighthouses begins with Dinko Fabris's reflection dedicated to the memory of Predrag Matvejević, the great Mediterranean scholar who, born in Mostar in 1932, died in Zagreb in 2017 after a life spent between asylum and exile from Yugoslavia to Paris and Rome. Furthermore, Fabris's reflection elaborates on the issue of geo-musicology, an interdisciplinary outreach of recent coinage that integrates musical expression, geo-political thinking, and the migratory movement of musicians in time and space. This book's itinerary follows then Fabris's opening chapter *Adriatic Geo-Musicology: A Premise* to Venice, the city many see as the womb of some kind of voracious aquatic monster that emerges from the Laguna, gives birth to the Adriatic Sea, and commingles birth, death, and rebirth in a dark cycle of immortality. This allegory fits the narrative of Chapter 2, *Tragedy and Hope in the Strait of Otranto*. In it, the author reflects on the story of a gondola, a battered patrol boat, and two musicians, framed in time and space between the Venetian Laguna and the Strait of Otranto, the geographic bookends of the Adriatic Sea.

The passing, along the Canal Grande, of a funeral gondola carrying the body of a young chorister to the Venetian cemetery on the island of San Michele, made a strong impression on an American traveler in 1876. His was a portentous sight that anticipated by six years the creation of a remarkable piano piece inspired by the passage along the Canal Grande of another funeral gondola, observed, that time, by Franz Liszt. He expressed his melancholia in *La lugubre gondola*, a piece he wrote in memory of the future: the impending death of Richard Wagner, his beloved father-in-law.

On March 28, 1997, in the Strait of Otranto, 430 nautical miles south of Venice, the Albanian vessel *Katër i Radës* was rammed and sunk by the Italian Navy. The vessel carried a clandestine human cargo of 122 people who had left the port of Vlöra in search of a better life in Italy. Eighty-one men, women, and children lost their lives in what was reported to be a most egregious breach of maritime protocol and, according to many, a deliberate criminal act on the part of the Italian government, carrying out its anti-immigration policies. The composer Admir Shkurtaj, an Albanian émigré, wrote a heartbreaking opera, *Katër i Radës, il naufragio*, in which he described vividly and dolefully the tragic migratory patterns that fate had forced upon his people. This one-act opera, commissioned by the 2014 Biennale di Venezia, premiered in Venice.

The Venetian Republic's culture, political savvy, diplomatic connivance, and military strategies form the backdrop of the rich panoply of people, music, influences, information, and events that made the island of Corfu, the Ionian Islands' administrative center and their preeminent step into the Adriatic Sea, a privileged crossroad between East and West, where cultures and religions meet, blend, and collide. In *Music Migrations and Creative Assimilations: The Ionian Islands* (Chapter 3), the Corfiot musicologist Kostas Kardamis discusses, among many migratory patterns to and from Corfu, the emergence of a Greek art music identity born out of the cultural merging that was forged on the island. Kardamis's documentation then extends north of the Ionian Islands toward the Dalmatian coast and joins the ethnomusicologist Jakša Primorac's intense comparative study of traditional choral settings, suggestively entitled *The Sailors' Chord: Comparative Research on Traditional Singing in the Quattro Province, the Ionian Islands, and Dalmatia* (Chapter 4). Primorac's study reveals remarkable structural similarities among popular choral settings practiced not only along the eastern Adriatic coast but in the Quattro Province area, located in the northwestern Apennines and along the Tyrrhenian Sea. It is extraordinary how the *cori d'osteria* (tavern choral songs) of the Quattro Province,[2] the *kantades, arietes*, and *arekia* of the Ionian Islands, and the Dalmatian *klapa* served to lift the communal spirit of thousands of people as they migrated from place to place. Their singing became then a sort of lingua franca, notwithstanding their different textual languages. In his research, Primorac employs a contemporary means of communication, YouTube, a novel and very efficacious comparative research tool.

Once the *cori d'osteria* have taken us to the western Apennines, the musicologist Francesco Zimei's reflection *Musicians on the Move in the Early Modern Era: An Instrumental Pilgrimage to L'Aquila* (Chapter 5) is set in the Abruzzi region across the Dalmatian coast. The author examines a trove of archival findings. These newly discovered documents concern the centuries-old tradition of instrumental music performed by musicians from all over Italy who gathered in the town of L'Aquila each year in May and August in the sixteenth century for the celebratory feasts in honor of Saint Peter Celestine. Complementing his historical narrative with strong archival, musical, and statistical documentation, the author pays particular attention to the sources of mid-Adriatic provenance—from Marche to northern Apulia, with emphasis on the Abruzzi, focusing on various instrumental combinations, their players, and possible repertoires.

Zimei's archival spirit also informs Maja Milošević's essay *The Migration of Seventeenth-Century Music Repertoire to the Cathedral of Hvar in Dalmatia* (Chapter 6), which takes us to the beautiful island of Hvar off the Dalmatian coast. Milošević's formidable archival research brings to light not only the migratory patterns established by the seventeenth century's musicians leading to and from the Venetian Republic but the actual "migration" of manuscripts and printed sheet music, which often preceded the presence on the island of composers and performers. These findings, writes the author, "serve as a strong and very rare evidence about musical practice in seventeenth century Hvar and Dalmatia in general."

Finally, regarding the eighteenth century, another distinguished Croatian musicologist, Vjera Katalinić provides, in Chapter 7, *Migration of Musicians as an Integrative Principle: The Case of the East Adriatic Coast in the Eighteenth Century*, a series of case studies conducted throughout the territories of Istria, the Croatian littoral, Dalmatia, and the Republic of Dubrovnik/Ragusa as part of the Italian/Mediterranean cultural circle. Although these lands lived through various political reconfigurations, they experienced a steadiness in terms of cultural issues. The constant need for educated musicians and repertoire for various occasions stimulated their migration in both directions: the locals searched for education in Italian centers, and Italian musicians searched for adequate jobs in eastern Adriatic towns and institutions. Katalinić's essay points to some models of migration as well as the specific merging of imported cultural layers with local traditions and needs in various aspects of musical life and culture, which were greatly facilitated by the internationalized musical style of the period.

The perplexing phenomenon of immigration is a double-edged sword; it enriches lives in the host countries while depleting the cultural capital of the lands left behind. Emigrants/immigrants are, more often than not, victims of rejection and unacceptance, a tragic reality that casts dark shadows over those who must live through them, including musicians, especially gifted individuals for whom the doors of the world's free societies should presumably always be open, as the language of music has need for neither words nor the verbalization of concepts. Musicians are magicians who perform wonders others cannot—even when tears overcome their smiles.

Acknowledgments

Edited volumes owe debts of gratitude to many people and institutions. However, in the case of this book, the editor and the contributing writers offer collective thanks to Professor Dinko Fabris, who, besides gracing this volume with his very eloquently documented opening chapter, has established the significance of geo-musicology and the path toward further studies in the field. Professor Fabris was the catalyst, in his role as president of the International Musicological Society, in securing a session at the conference *Musicians in the Mediterranean: Narratives of Movement* (Naples, 21–26 June 2016) where the writers of this volume could meet, exchange their ideas, present their papers, and plan this volume.

Second, thanks are due to the College Music Society's Board of Editors and Professor Todd Sullivan in particular for encouraging the idea of a collection of essays on musicians' migratory patterns along and across the Adriatic Sea. Also, I thank Professor Juan Chattah, at the University of Miami, for offering a much-appreciated critical appraisal of draft ideas. The project moved then to a second phase: the publishing aspects of a book that could serve to launch the new CMS-Cultural Expressions in Music Series, published by Routledge. Constance Ditzel, Senior Editor of Music at Routledge, has been exceptional in guiding the project toward fruition, including the reshaping of its format to suit the new editorial vision for the series as a more agile, synthetic source of information.

Finally, on a personal note, I wish to offer thanks to my wife, Louise Cavanaugh Sciannameo, for having "lived" the stories that compose this book and for having constantly provided her editorial acumen in shaping the overall narrative.

Franco Sciannameo
August 2017
Pittsburgh, Pennsylvania

Notes

1. For comprehensive political, geographical and cultural views of the Adriatic established by Pierre Cabanes, Olivier Chaline, Bernard Doumerc, Alain Ducellier, and Michel Sivignon, see their *Histoire de l'Adriatique* (Paris: Étidion du Seuil, 2001). An Italian version of this book was published under the title *Storia dell'Adriatico* by Il lavoro editoriale (Ancona, 2014).
2. Quattro Province include the provinces of Alessandria (Piemonte), Genova (Liguria), Pavia (Lombardia), and Piacenza (Emilia-Romagna).

1 Adriatic Geo-Musicology

A Premise

Dinko Fabris

The frontispiece of *Viaggio in Dalmazia dell'Abate Alberto Fortis*, published in Venice in 1774, bears the author's inserted motto after Macrobius's *Commentary* on Cicero's *Somnium Scipionis*, which he obviously liked. It reads, "in this very part of the world, wisdom could last forever but it does not, because, either by conflagration or cataclysmic flood, it will be swept away by the twilight of the long existence of things."[1]

Through the centuries, Mediterranean people grew accustomed to natural cataclysms and wars, especially in the narrow waters of the Adriatic Sea where the Levantine Italian coast and a land known as Dalmatia are separated by only 100 miles. Since the ancient Greeks, people of various origin brought in turn destruction and the markings of faraway civilizations, and, in Alberto Fortis's time, the centuries-old (and ambiguous) tension between Venetians and Ottomans was still ablaze. As always, geopolitics generated inevitable consequences in the artistic and musical histories of those lands.

Since the earliest Greek colonial expeditions, ever moving north of the Adriatic—after centuries of excursions along the waters on the part of merchant ships and adventurers in search of raw material—one can understand the presence of only a few "technical" ports along the Adriatic coasts, pointing more toward the riches of the southern Italian peninsula, where the "Magna Grecia" was established, than toward other territories, which remained unexplored for a long time. Aside from the narrow passage between Otranto and Corfu (barely 70 kilometers) or that between Vlöra and the actual Apulia, "merchant vessels directed toward the emporia of the Padan Delta for the purchase of cereals and metals sailed the Adriatic along the coast of Dalmatia, perhaps as far as Zara from where they continued the journey through Mount Conero, then along the littoral of Romagna," wrote Francesco Prontera.[2]

After the fall of the Roman Empire, several civilizations and religions sometimes blended or coexisted harmoniously. At other times, they fought each other furiously. Ships, however, continued to follow an obligatory zig-zag route along the narrow Adriatic waters.

When the invasions of barbaric hordes overwhelmed the territories under Roman administration that extended to the Adriatic coast, resulting in the birth of Venice, the Adriatic people looked for safety to far away Byzantium.[3]

Around the year 1000, Bari, a city on the south of the Italian peninsula, became an emblem of tolerance because of its multilayered governmental structures and religious diversity: a Byzantium dependent since the separation of the two Roman Empires and yet the seat of a Saracen Emirate between 847 and 871 while under the influence of the Longobard Duchy of Benevento.[4] Kalfàn, the first emir, decided to use the paleo-Christian cathedral as a mosque, thus reserving the respective sacred days for their rites on Fridays for the Arabs, Saturdays for the Jews (who maintained a strong presence in the whole of Apulia), and Sundays for the Christians.

Once the seat was restored as a Byzantine Katapano, the city was conquered by the Normans, then the Swabians, and finally the Angevins, notwithstanding its ties to and strong commercial interests in Venice, which had saved Bari from a new Saracen siege in 1002. The city's fundamental event was the erection of the basilica for the preservation of Saint Nicholas's bones, which some fishermen from Bari had stolen and smuggled from Myrna, in Asia Minor, in 1087. The church quickly became one of the most important pilgrimage destinations on the way to Jerusalem and was particularly dear to the Slavic populations. In fact, members of the Serbian Nemanidi dynasty in the thirteenth century appear immortalized in the icons currently preserved in the Saint Nicholas Basilica. Bari, therefore, witnessed the frequent visits of Serbian monarchs until close to our times.

I cited this case not only because of the currently burning topic of "tolerance" but because it had noticeable consequences in the field of musical studies as well. Aside from the precocious fusions of practices of religious singing differently due to the alternate use of the same site of cult (as one can still observe nowadays in the *Santo Sepolcro* in Jerusalem), a *scriptorium* was created in the monastery annexed to the Saint Nicholas Basilica in Bari as a school for writing Christian chants, which resulted in some of the excellent masterpieces of musical notation identified by specialists as "Bari-type." This type of notation is identical to that used in liturgical codices found on the other side of the Adriatic, namely in Ragusa (now Dubrovnik), Split, and Zadar.[5]

The same type of writing assumed different connotations in the hands of the monk Giovanni da Oppido, educated perhaps at the Bari *scriptorium* and converted to Judaism under the name of Obadiah. From 1102 on, he moved east, visiting the cities of Aleppo, Damascus, Tyro, and Palestine before ending his existence in Egypt. There, a fragmented version of his autobiography containing the first examples of Hebrew chants written in the "Bari-type" notation, which was read from right to left, was found.[6]

After the fall of Constantinople in 1453, a strong migratory wave of Christians fled the advance of the Turks—generically defined as "Albanians," like the two "Oriental" male protagonists of Mozart's *Così fan tutte*—so we find in Apulia and the inland region of Basilicata entire ethnic groups called Arbëreschë, that is, "Albanians of Italy," who kept, over the centuries, besides the language, a Greco-Byzantine religious rite and partly archaic music traditions as well. Until recent times, a traditional use of instruments on the part of these communities reveal the use of instruments whose provenance is attributed to the other coast of the Adriatic. See, for instance, the *làhuta*, a chordophone akin to the Slavic *gusla* (however, its name recalls the lute, an instrument present in both European and Ottoman traditions), and the *surdulìna*, a small bagpipe known in southern Italy at the time of the Aragonese domination as "sordellina."[7] An Albanian named Prente played *cetra* and *ceterone* at the annual summer festivities of *del Perdono* in the Abruzzi city of L'Aquila during the period 1543–1571.[8] In the eighteenth century, the chants of the Albanians of Italy acquired a literary preeminence for some times due, perhaps, to nostalgic feelings toward Albania's national hero, George Castriot, known as Skanderbeg.[9]

Exchanges of music and musicians between the Adriatic coasts remained strong throughout the time when Venice and the Ottomans disputed their control over the lands while pirates from diverse nations and religions terrorized the small coastal towns.[10] In the first half of the sixteenth century, the lute virtuoso Giacomo Gorzanis, an "Apulian," emigrated to the north in search of work, became a citizen of Trieste, and, despite his blindness, worked intensely for Slovenian patrons as well as for the Bavarian court.[11] A century later, another emigrant musician, Enrico Radesca from Foggia, joined the Venetian Army and fought in Dalmatia against the Turks before obtaining employment at the Court of Turin, where he acquired fame through his numerous printed collections of monodies and madrigals.[12]

Naturally, Venice was the protagonist of all major artistic and cultural exchanges between the two coasts of the Adriatic for almost one thousand years. But, it was not alone, because the Adriatic was transited continually by ships bearing flags of all nationalities (aside from the pirates). The proud maritime Republic of Ragusa (now Dubrovnik) won distinction for its cultural vivacity. Although the earthquake of 1667 hampered the revival of its Renaissance and Baroque splendor, throughout the eighteenth century the Republic of Ragusa was a preeminent musical center, as Italian musicians of the Neapolitan school were invited to teach promising Dalmatian musicians, who acquired a fame of their own, such as the members of the Sorkočević family.[13]

Numerous were the musical centers located along the coast, especially where the Venetians established a cultured ruling class. While the cathedral of Lesina (now the island of Hvar)[14] hosted prestigious Italian musicians traveling from Pirano, Zadar, and Split, others, like Giuseppe Tartini, Michele Stratico, and Giulio Bjamonti, moved to Padua.[15] However, it was Venice that created, above all, an efficient network among small Italian-style theaters, in its so-called *da mar* territories. Such theaters served initially to showcase the influence and affluence of local elites and later were obligatory stops for the many touring theatrical companies that made the rounds of the three seas surrounding the network: the Adriatic, the Ionian, and the Aegean.

The cities possessing Venetian-style theaters were aligned along the Italian coast from Veneto to Apulia and on the opposite side in the principal centers of Zadar, Split, Hvar, Dubrovnik, Kotor, and then Corfu and the other Greek islands all the way to Anatolia.[16] Arrived in Smyrna in 1841, shortly after a disastrous fire, the Italian Giuseppe Francesco Baruffi marveled at the passion for the theater and the Italian language he found in that city "busy building two new theaters to replace those destroyed by fire: one dedicated to Italian opera with a capacity of 500 seats, and the other to French comedies and vaudevilles," he wrote.[17] It was in Smyrna, the "Home of Homer," that Baruffi heard "some blind Greeks singing in the streets about daily events in elegant popular poetry" and improvising verses on the recent fire accident.[18] This is another characteristic that strongly tied people of diverse religions and backgrounds from the heart of the Adriatic to the eastern Mediterranean: the presence of singing storytellers. We encounter them (often blind and analphabet) under different names and playing different instruments (generally strings) in Crete as well as Anatolia, among the Kurds in Lebanon and Syria, in Palestine, and in many Arab territories. The most noted example is Avdo Mededović, the "Yugoslav Homer," considered by Milman Parry and Albert Lord as "the most cultivated" of all the Slavic "guslari" who were phono recorded in the years 1933–1935 and 1950–1951.[19]

Singing with accompaniment of the *gusla* (a type of popular viola bearing a zoomorphic head and one or two strings played with a bow) brings us back to the voyage in Dalmatia of Alberto Fortis, because the only extended musical description found in his book of 1774 is dedicated to the "guzia" singers known as "Morlacchi" (a definition still in use to indicate people whose manners are uncultured and rough).[20]

Fortis paid a tribute of gratitude to Giulio (Julije) Bajamonti, the musician and theoretician from Split, for the precious ethnographic information he received. Bajamonti, for his part, published an article titled "Il morlacchismo d'Omero" in 1797.[21] The Italian musicologist Ivano Cavallini has demonstrated that sort of "Morlakmania" that pervaded the literature and even Italian opera throughout the nineteenth century. It identified *tout court* the Morlacks with Slav people, primitive singers, and players descended from Homer, a perfect Mediterranean alternative to the north European Ossian bard.[22]

An analogous phenomenon was noted by the "appearance" of the "Turk" as a theatrical character, in Venetian operas first and in Italian operas later in the seventeenth century. At the beginning, the "Turk" was morally attacked and ridiculed because of his fearfulness—as the Ottomans appeared to be unstoppable—but then the character was gradually toned down and reduced to a mask. Recent musicological studies have paid attention to this case.[23] However, the obligatory starting point concerning the relations between the West and the Middle East is still the classic volume *Orientalism* by Edward Said, which still awaits a properly sufficient response from musicologists.[24]

Notwithstanding the burgeoning appearance of international collaborations, especially connected to European institutions, a full study of the musical relations between the two coasts of the Adriatic was not attempted until the making of this volume, a brainchild of Franco Sciannameo. It will become evident through the reading of these essays that the book's goal is not to find similitudes and analogies according to the modes of the old "*musicologie comparée*," which gave birth to ethnomusicology, but to enrich the knowledge of historical musicology, particularly in regard to this geographic territory interconnected through the centuries by means of information different from the usual, that is, not limited to written sources or archival documents. There are travelers' chroniclers, iconographic representations, sound recordings, and so on that offer an extraordinary reconstruction of a plausible Adriatic soundscape, in its salient historical moments.

In 2002, Franco Alberto Gallo launched the idea of creating "a new discipline, a sort of musical geography complementary to the traditional history of music."[25] Around Gallo's idea of "music geography," a study group hailing from the University of Bologna was created. This group is now under the leadership of Donatella Restani and Nicoletta Guidobaldi, (former pupils and followers of Gallo), whose goal is to examine the enormous amount of travel literature throughout times and places, using the double lens of musicological scrutiny and ethnomusicological empiricism combined, in order to restore a historical narrative pertinent to the "people without notes."[26]

Venice, Marco Polo's point of departure and the end of the Silk Road, is also a protagonist in this field because of its innumerable sources, starting with the large travel literature since the time of Ramusio in the sixteenth century.[27]

I find the idea of geo-musicology particularly fitting to explore the history of musical relations between the Adriatic coasts because it responds to the most important lacuna that has emerged from the investigation of the soundscape, which is also connected to a geography of music: urban musicology as currently practiced and limited, by definition, to the study of urban landscapes.[28]

The Adriatic, the point of departure for an ideal circumnavigation of the Mediterranean, is a complex of coasts, islands, peninsulas, ports, rivers, and promontories and mountains in the hinterlands, home to an infinite variety of people, as explained by the best guide available thus far: Predrag Matveivić's *Mediterranean: A Cultural Landscape*.[29]

I am sure that this book will be a major contribution to the Adriatic geo-musicology project, based on water and stories rather than documents/ monuments. On the other hand, the forced dynamism of the Adriatic people has truly anticipated the idea of "liquid society" as advanced by Zygmunt Bauman.

Notes

1. See *Viaggio in Dalmazia dell'Abate Alberto Fortis*, Venezia, Alvise Milocco all'Apolline, 1774, 2 vols. (copy consulted at A–Wn). Available online: www.larici.it/itinerari/allegati/fortis-dalmazia.pdf. Also, see modern edition edited by Eva Viani (Venezia: Marsilio, 1987).
2. See Francesco Prontera, "Le comunicazioni maritime," in *I Greci in Occidente*, catalogo della Mostra di Venezie 1996, edited by Giovanni Pugliese Carratelli (Milano: Bompiani, 1996), 201–208: 204.
3. See *L'Adriatico dalla tarda antichità all'età carolingia*. Atti del convegno di Brescia 11–13 ottobre 2001, a cura di Gian Pietro Brogiolo a Paolo Delogu (Firenze: All'insegna del Giglio, 2005).
4. See Nino Lavermicocca, *Bari Bizantina: capitale mediterranea* (Bari: Edizioni di Pagina, 2003). For details on music in the Bari area, see Dinko Fabris, "Vita musicale a Bari dal medioevo al Settecento," in *La musica a Bari: Dalle cantorie medioevali al Conservatorio Piccinni*, a cura di Dinko Fabris e Marco Renzi, con un intervento di Riccardo Muti (Bari: Levante, 1993), 19–108.
5. Regarding exchanges of medieval liturgical repertoire between the two Adriatic coasts, see the CD *Terra Adriatica* ("Croatian and Italian Medieval sacred music"), performed and produced by the singer and musicologist Katarina Livljanic and her ensemble, Dialogos (L'Empreinte Digitale, ED 13 107, 2002).
6. Fragments of Obadiah's autobiography and the pages containing music notation have been reproduced in *Giovanni-Ovodiah da Oppido proselito, viaggiatore e musicista dell'età normanna*, atti del convegno di Oppido Lucano 28–30 marzo 2004, a cura di Antonio De Rosa e Mauro Perani (Firenze: Giuntina, 2005).
7. For more information on this instrument and related performative context, see Nicola Scaldaferri, *Musica arbëreshe in Basilicata* (Lecce: Adriatica Editrice Salentina, 1994).
8. See Francesco Zimei, *I "cantici" del Perdono: Laude e soni nella devozione aquilana a San Pietro Celestino* (Lucca: LIM, 2015), 339 and 499.
9. See Girolamo De Rada, *Rapsodie d'un poema Albanese raccolte nelle colonie del napoletano* (Firenze: Tipografia di Federico Bencini, 1866).

10. There is a large bibliography on pirate activities along the Adriatic, which has remained untapped by musicology. See, for example, Lorenzo Braccesi, *La pirateria nell'Adriatico antico* (Roma: L'Erma di Bretschneider, 2004); Stevka Šmitran, *Gli Uscocchi: Pirati, ribelli, guerrieri tra gli imperi ottoman e asburgico e la Repubblica di Venezia* (Venezia: Marsilio, 2008); Sante Graciotti (ed.), *Mito e antimito di Venezia nel bacino Adriatico: Secoli XV–XIX*, a cura di Sante Graciotti (Roma: Il Calamo–Venezia, Fondazione Giorgio Cini, 2001).

11. See Alenka Bagarič, *"Villanelle alla napolitana" Giacoma Gorzanisa in njego vavloga v siritvi vilanele iz Italjena Kranjsko in v sosednje avstrijske dezele*, PhD dissertation (University of Ljubljana, 2009), with Bibliography. Giacomo Gorzanis's Opera Omnia are currently in publication in the series "Monumenta Artis Musicae Slovenje." Thus far the following volumes are available: 51. *Il primo libro di napolitane (1570) . . . Il secondo libro delle napolitane a tre voci (1571)* (2007); 53. *Intabulatura di liuto Libro primo (1561)* (2011); 58. *Il secondo libro de intabulatura di liuto (1562)* (2014).

12. Radesca mentioned his military service in a dedication to Zeno, the Venetian ambassador, of his *Libro primo di madrigali* (Venezia, 1615). Since a manuscript preserved at the Biblioteca Queriniana in Brescia contains some *canzonette spirituali* by "Simone Radesca," I assume that the musician could have had a name of Jewish or perhaps Dalmatian origin, as Rado, Grado, Gradisca appear in the toponymy of the Slavic coast. Furthermore, I noticed that a certain "caporal Simon" is mentioned in a composition inserted in the Op. IV of Marco Uccellini (*Sonate, correnti, et arie*, op. 4, 1645) titled *Aria XI sopra il "Caporal Simon"*: see Dinko Fabris, "Enrico Radesca e i musicisti nati in Puglia," in *Enrico Radesca di Foggia e il suo tempo*, a cura di Francesca Seller (Lucca: LIM, 2001), 59–76: 72.

13. See Vjera Katalinić, *The Sorkocevices: Aristocratic Musicians from Dubrovnik* (Zagreb: Croatian Music Information Centre, 2014). This text includes a CD with music of the *Sorkočévic* family.

14. See Maja Milošević, "The Town of Hvar as the Meeting Point of Musicians in the 17th and 18th Centuries," in *Music Migrations in the Early Modern Age: People, Markets, Patterns and Styles*, edited by Vjera Katalinić (Zagreb: HDM [Croatian Musicological Society], 2016), 103–117. Also, see Milošević's contribution in this volume.

15. The bibliography regarding these musicians, Tartini in particular, is too vast to be discussed here. Therefore, I suggest a number of recent studies that contain pertinent bibliographic information: Metoda Kokole and Alenka Bagarić, *La musica veneziana nell'Istria settentrionale*, Catalogo della Mostra di Ljubljana 2014, a cura di Metoda Kokole in collaborazione con Alenka Bagarić (Ljubljana: Zalozba Zrc, 2014); Metoda Kokole and Michael Talbot (eds.), "Giuseppe Tartini and Research into His Life, Works and Time," special issue of the periodical *De musica disserenda* [Ljubljana, Institute of Musicology] 10/1 (2014); Stanislav Tuksar (ed.), *Zagreb and Croatian Lands, as a Bridge between Central European and Mediterranean Musical Cultures*, Proceedings of the Symposium Xgreb 1994 (Zabreb: HMD [Croatian Musicological Society], 1998). A useful introduction to music in Dalmatia can be found still in Josip Andreis, *Music in Croatia* [1974], second enlarged edition (Zagreb: Institute of Musicology, 1982). Further studies are available in Katalinić (ed.), *Music Migrations in the Early Modern Age*. Finally, for musical exchanges between Istria and Italy since the Renaissance, see Ivano Cavallini, *Musica, cultura e spettacolo in Istria tra '500 e '600* (Firenze: Olschki/Venezia, Fondazione Giorgio Cini, 1990).

16. The history of the Italian opera companies that traveled along the Adriatic and Mediterranean routes waits to be written. An idea signaling the richness of this field of research can be drawn from John Rosselli's *L'impresario d'opera* (Torino: EDT, 1985), 185–: "exemplar were the father-son agents Antonio and Alessandro Magotti whose activity in Bologna covered the nineteenth century from 1820 on. They provided companies . . . to small towns like Adria, Medicina or Spoleto, and Bari or Martina Franca in Apulia, Greek cities like Corfu and Patrasso where Italian operas were performed regularly. Often, they assumed impresario roles in 1879 when Alessandro Magotti guaranteed by a certain date the arrival in Corfu of a full company complete with music and wardrobe. In sum, the agent assumed a more solid importance than the impresario."

17. See Giuseppe Francesco Baruffi, *Pellegrinazioni autunnali ed opuscoli: Il presente volume contiene il viaggio da Torino a Costantinopoli attraverso la Grecia, nell'anno 1841* (Torino: Cassone e Marzorati, 1842), 133. This book was particularly well received and was reprinted under the title *Viaggio in Oriente* several times starting with its 1847 Milan edition.

18. Ibid., 134.

19. Albert B. Lord, *The Singer of Tales* [1960], second edition by Stephen Mitchell and Gregory Nagy (Cambridge, MA: Harvard University Press, 2000). For an analogous tradition in Albania and the relationships between singers/storytellers from different area of the Balkans, see Nicola Scadaferri, "Itinerari di frontiera: I canti epici albanesi nel contesto dell'epica balcanica," in *L'eredità di Diego Carpitella: Etnomusicologia, antropologia e ricerca storica nel Salento e nell'area mediterranea*, a cura di Maurizio Agamennone e Gino L. Di Mitri (Nardò: Besa, 2003), 93–111.

20. Fortis, *Viaggio in Dalmazia, Costumi de' Morlacchi*, §14, "Musica e poesia," 88.

21. See Marco Martin, "Giulio Bajamonti e le Narodne Pjesme della tradizione dei guslari dalmato-bosniaci," in *Per una soria dei popoli senza note*, a cura di Paola Dessi (Padova: CLUEB, 2010), 190–207 (with many references to Fortis's *Viaggio in Dalmazia*).

22. Ivano Cavallini, "From the Morlack to the Slav: Images of South Slavic People between Exoticism and Illyrism in Italian Literature and Opera during the 19th Century," in *Nation and/or Homeland: Identity in 19th Century Music and Literature between Central and Mediterranean Europe*, edited by Ivano Cavallini (Milano-Udine: Mimesis, 2012), 103–123.

23. Mustafa Soykut, "Image of the 'Turk' in Italy: A History of the 'Other,'" in *Early Modern Europe, 1453–1683* (Berlin: Klaus Schwarz Verlag, 2001); Matthew W. Read, *Orientalism, Masquerade and Mozart's Turkish Music* (London: Royal Music Association, 2000) (RMA Monographs, 9); Michael Hüttler and Hans Ernst Weidenger (eds.), *Ottoman Empire and European Theatre, Vol. 1: The Age of Mozart and Selim III (1756–1808)* (Vienna: Hollitzer Wissenschaftsverlag, 2013); Ralph P. Locke, *Music and the Exotic from the Renaissance to Mozart* (Cambridge: Cambridge University Press, 2015). A section of the International Conference *Music in the Mediterranean Diaspora* (Florence, Villa I Tatti, 18–19 March 2017) was dedicated to the cross visions between Europe and the Ottoman Empire. Conference proceedings, edited by Kate van Order, are forthcoming. A particularly sad case regarding the image of the "Turkish personage" reflects the emotional reaction generated in Europe by the assassination, ordered in 1635, by the Ottoman Sultan Murad IV of his younger brothers

Bayezid and Süleyman. This assassination became the subject of tragedies and operas for decades during the seventeenth century. Regarding Luigi Rossi's version of the story in his cantata *Rugge quasi leon*, see Rana Íren, *Early Orientalism: Roman Sing the Ottomans in* Rugge quasi leon *by Luigi Rossi*, master's thesis (Istambul Technical University, 2016).

24. Edward Said, *Orientalism* [1978], 25th anniversary edition with a new preface by the author (New York: Vintage Books, 2003). I suggest here a few texts thus far available: John M. MacKenzie, *Orientalism: History, Theory and the Arts* (Manchester: Manchester University Press, 1995); Nasser Al-Taee, *Representations of the Orient in Western Music: Violence and Sensuality* (Farnham: Ashgate, 2010); Rachel Beckles Willson, *Orientalism and Musical Mission: Palestine and the West* (Cambridge: Cambridge University Press, 2013).

25. "Il me semble qu'il serait fort intéressant de créer une nouvelle discipline, une sorte de géographie de la musique qui pourrait compléter l'histoire de la musique traditionnelle": Franco Alberto Gallo, "Voyages croisés: Musique, musiciens, artistes et voyageurs entre France et Italie au XVe siècle," in *Regards croisés: Musiques, musiciens, artistes et voyageurs entre France et Italie au XVe siècle* (Tours: Minerve, 2002), 171 ("Epitome musicale").

26. See Franco Alberto Gallo, "Premessa," in *Per una soria dei popoli senza note*, a cura di Paola Dessi (Padova: CLUEB, 2010), 7–10. The Bologna Study Group has published its findings in various journals, including *Musica e storia* (Venezia: Fondazione Levi) and *Itineraria: Travel Literature and Knowledge of the World from Antiquity to the Renaissance* (Firenze: I: 2002). Vol. 16 of *Inineraria* (2017) is dedicated to the panel "The Eye (and the Ear) of Travellers: Mediterranean Routes," which took place at the Joint Conference IMS/ICTM *Musicians of the Mediterranean: Narratives of Movement* (Naples, 21–25 June 2016).

27. See Giovanni Battista Ramusio, *Navigazioni e viaggi*, a cura di Marisa Milanesi, 6 vols. (Torino: Einaudi, 1978–1983). The Archivio di Stato in Venice provides the largest repository of information on the history of traveling and daily life along the Adriatic through the end of the nineteenth century; see *Guida generale degli Archivi di Stato Italiani. Archivio di Venezia* (Roma: Ministero Beni Culturali, 1994). In particular, see the reports marked "da mar," which contains documents on Istria, Dalmatia, Uscocchi, Levant, "Adriatic Navigation," and embassies and consulates. Also very important is the series of documents marked "Documenti turchi," which can be consulted in *'I Documenti Turchi' dell'Archivio di Stato di Venezia*, a cura di Maria Pia Pedani Fabris e Alessio Bombaci (Roma: Ministero per i Beni Culturali e Ambiantali, 1994) and *Inventory of the 'Lettere e scritture turchesche' in the Venetian State Archives*, edited by Maria Pia Pedani Fabris (Leiden-Boston: Brill, 2010).

28. I have elaborated upon this problem in my article "Urban Musicologies," an Introduction to *Hearing the City in Early Modern Europe*, Proceedings of the ICREA International Workshop *Hearing the City: Musical Experiences as Portal to Urban Soundscapes* (Barcelona, 24–26 September 2015), edited by Tess Knighton and Ascensión Mazuela-Anguita (Tournhout: Brepols, 2017).

29. Predrag Matvejević, *Mediterranean: A Cultural Landscape* (Berkeley: University of California Press, 1999). The original text was published in 1987 in Serbo-Croatian (Zagreb: GZH) and in Italian (Milano: Hefti) under the title *Mediterranski Brevijar/Breviario Mediterraneo* (the Italian book includes an Introduction by Claudio Magris, an eminent scholar of Adriatic culture and

literature). I shared with Pedrag Matvejević many conversations about our common biographical experience, Pedrag being a Serbia born in Mostar in the former Yugoslavia and forced to live as an exile between Paris and Italy. My Veneto-Italian family was transplanted in Zadar first and later on the island of Hvar and then was compelled to flee Dalmatia during the Second World War and move to unoccupied Italy, the city of Bari, where I was born.

References

Agamennone, Maurizio and Gino L. Di Mitri, eds. *L'eredità di Diego Carpitella. Etnomusicologia, antropologia e ricerca storica nel Salento e nell'area mediterranea*. Nardò: Besa, 2003.

Al-Taee, Nasser. *Representations of the Orient in Western Music: Violence and Sensuality*. Farnham: Ashgate, 2010.

Andreis, Josip. *Music in Croatia* [1974], second enlarged edition. Zagreb: Institute of Musicology, 1982.

Beckles, Wilson and Rachel Beckles. *Orientalism and Musical Mission: Palestine and the West*. Cambridge: Cambridge University Press, 2013.

Braccesi, Lorenzo. *La pirateria nell'Adriatico antico*. Roma: L'Erma di Bretschneider, 2004.

Cavallini, Ivano. *Musica, cultura e spettacolo in Istria tra '500 e '600*. Firenze: Olschki/Venezia, Fondazione Giorgio Cini, 1990.

———, ed. *Nation and/or Homeland: Identity in 19th Century Music and Literature between Central and Mediterranean Europe*. Milano-Udine: Mimesis, 2012.

Dessi, Paola, ed. *Per una soria dei popoli senza note*. Padova: CLUEB, 2010: 190–207 (with Many References to Fortis's *Viaggio in Dalmazia*).

Graciotti, Sante, ed. *Mito e antimito di Venezia nel bacino Adriatico: secoli XV–XIX*. Roma: Il Calamo–Venezia, Fondazione Giorgio Cini, 2001.

Hüttler, Michael and Hans Ernst Weidenger, eds. *Ottoman Empire and European Theatre, Vol. 1: The Age of Mozart and Selim III (1756–1808)*. Vienna: Hollitzer Wissenschaftsverlag, 2013.

Katalinić, Vjera. *The Sorkovecives: Aristocratic Musicians from Dubrovnik*. Zagreb: Croatian Music Information Centre, 2014.

Kokole, Metoda and Alenka Bagarić. *La musica veneziana nell'Istria settentrionale*. Ljubljana: Zalozba Zrc, 2014 (Catalogo della Mostra di Ljubljana 2014).

Kokole, Metoda and Michael Talbot, eds. "Giuseppe Tartini and Research into His Life, Works and Time." Special issue of the periodical *De musica disserenda* [Ljubljana, Institute of Musicology] 10/1, 2014.

Lavermicocca, Nino. *Bari Bizantina: capitale mediterranea*. Bari: Edizioni di Pagina, 2003.

Locke, Ralph P. *Music and the Exotic from the Renaissance to Mozart*. Cambridge: Cambridge University Press, 2015.

Lord, Albert B. *The Singer of Tales* [1960], second edition by Stephen Mitchell and Gregory Nagy. Cambridge, MA: Harvard University Press, 2000.

MacKenzie, John M. *Orientalism: History, Theory and the Arts*. Manchester: Manchester University Press, 1995.

Matvejević, Predrag. *Mediterranean: A Cultural Landscape.* Berkeley: University of California Press, 1999. The original text was published in 1987 in Serbo-Croatian (Zagreb: GZH) and in Italian (Milano: Hefti) under the title *Mediterranski Brevijar/Breviario Mediterraneo* (the Italian book includes an Introduction by Claudio Magris).

Pedani Fabris, Maria Pia, ed. *Inventory of the 'Lettere e scritture turchesche' in the Venetian State Archives.* Leiden-Boston: Brill, 2010.

Pedani Fabris, Maria Pia and Alessio Bombaci, eds. *'I Documenti Turchi' dell'Archivio di Stato di Venezia.* Rome: Ministero per i Beni Culturali e Ambiantali, 1994.

Ramusio, Giovanni Battista. *Navigazioni e viaggi.* a cura di Marisa Milanesi, 6 vols., Torino: Einaudi, 1978–1983.

Read, Matthew W. *Orientalism, Masquerade and Mozart's Turkish Music.* London: Royal Music Association, 2000 (RMA Monographs, 9).

Rosselli, John. *L'impresario d'opera.* Torino: EDT, 1985.

Said, Edward. *Orientalism* [1978], 25th Anniversary edition with a new preface by the Author. New York: Vintage Books, 2003.

Scaldaferri, Nicola. *Musica arbëreshe in Basilicata.* Lecce: Adriatica Editrice Salentina, 1994.

Seller, Francesca, ed. *Enrico Radesca di Foggia e il suo tempo.* Lucca: LIM, 2001.

Šmitran, Stevka. *Gli Uscocchi: pirati, ribelli, guerrieri tra gli imperi ottoman e asburgico e la Repubblica di Venezia.* Venezia: Marsilio, 2008.

Tuksar, Stanislav, ed. *Zagreb and Croatian Lands, as a Bridge between Central European and Mediterranean Musical Cultures.* Proceedings of the Symposium Xgreb 1994. Zabreb: HMD [Croatian Musicological Society], 1998.

Zimei, Francesco. *I 'cantici' del Perdono: Laude e soni nella devozione aquilana a San Pietro Celestino.* Lucca: LIM, 2015.

2 Tragedy and Hope in the Strait of Otranto

Franco Sciannameo

A Funeral in Venice

I happened to witness a picturesque funeral in Venice. It was that of a chorus-
boy, in a church on one of the smaller canals somewhere west of the Rialto. I
stumbled on the church accidentally that forenoon, and was not able to find
it again the next day—a circumstance to which the incident perhaps owes
the fairy-like atmosphere that envelops it for me. The building had disap-
peared, like Aladdin's palace, in the night. They were performing a mass
as I entered. The great rose window behind the organ and the chancel windows were darkened with draperies, and the colossal candles were burning.
The coffin, covered with a heavily-embroidered pall, stood on an elevated
platform in front of the magnificent altar. The inlaid columns glistening in
the candle-light, the smoke of the incense curling lazily up to the frescoed
dome, the priests in elaborate robes kneeling around the bier—it was like a
masterly composed picture. When the ceremonies were concluded, the coffin was lifted from the platform by six young friars and borne to a gondola
in waiting at the steps near the portals. The priests, carrying a huge golden
crucifix and several tail gilt torches, unlighted, crowded into the bow and
stern of the floating hearse, which was attached by a long rope to another
gondola occupied by caremen. Following these were two or three covered
gondolas whose connection with the obsequies was not clear to me, as they
appeared to be empty. Slowly down the narrow canal, in that dead stillness
which reigns in Venice, swept the somber flotilla, bearing its unconscious
burden to the Campo Santo. The air was full of vagrant Spring scents, and
the sky that arched over all was carved of one vast, unclouded turquoise. In
the deserted church were two old crones scraping up the drippings of the
wax candles from the tessellated pavement. Nothing except time is wasted
in Italy.

These impressions were reported by an unidentified traveler to Venice in
the *Atlantic Monthly* issue for December 1876. Six years later, Franz Liszt
began thinking about spending the winter of 1882 in Venice at the sumptu-
ous Palazzo Vendramin, the home of his daughter Cosima and her husband,

Richard Wagner. Liszt stayed in Venice from November 19, 1882, to January 13, 1883. Wagner died a month after Liszt's departure.

Richard and Cosima had leased the second floor of Palazzo Vendramin for one year. It belonged to Duca della Grazia, who had kept the original furnishings, paintings, and carpets in luxurious condition. The Wagner family's quarters occupied 18 rooms assigned to Richard, Cosima, their four children, three tutors, four domestic servants, and two gondoliers. The gondoliers had become a vital part of the household, since the only access to the palazzo was along the waterways, and the gondoliers provided a continuous ferry service for the family and their guests. A spacious apartment had been set aside for Liszt's own use, and he was free to come and go as he pleased. He had not known a real family life for many years; he often joined the Wagner family for their meals and enjoyed relaxing among his grandchildren and generally being looked after by Cosima, wrote Alan Walker.[1]

Palazzo Vendramin overlooked the Canal Grande, and from its windows Liszt re-experienced the magic of Venice that had haunted him since his first visit, in 1837. This time, though, Palazzo Vendramin and the Canal Grande turned into a portent of death: Wagner was mortally ill. When Liszt happened to observe a funeral procession of gondolas moving gently along the Canal Grande on its way to the cemetery on the island of San Michele, he experienced a choking feeling of foreboding and, turning away from the window, retreated to the piano to pour over the keyboard his most daring thoughts aimed at "freezing" death; a short composition was born, and he called it *La lugubre gondola*.[2]

Years later, Venice, queen of the Adriatic, a city where death, carnival, and migration of souls are inextricably intertwined, gave birth to a heart-wrenching opera, *Katër i Radës, il naufragio* by the Albanian composer Admir Shkurtaj. This one-act opera with a libretto by Alessandro Leogrande possessed the power to transport the audience attending its premiere at the 2014 Biennale di Venezia from the placid waters of the Laguna to the depths of the Strait of Otranto, the Serenissima's historical point of access to and from the Mediterranean Sea. At some 15 miles off the Albanian coast, the souls of 81 dead immigrant men, women, and children implore their gods for justice and redemption; Admir Shkurtaj has given them a voice!

This chapter reflects upon a tragic event that took place on Good Friday, March 28, 1997, at the nearest distance point between the east and west coasts of the Adriatic Sea where cultures and religions meet, blend, and collide.

Admir Shkurtaj was born in Tirana, Albania, in 1969, to parents in the employ of the Albanian government; his father was an officer in the army and his mother an executive of the Labor Party. Admir, his older brother, and a younger sister grew up somewhat sheltered by the fatalistic sense of security dictatorial regimes provide. At a very young age he learned music from an uncle, a blind accordion player, then took regular accordion lessons at the Jordan Misja music school, followed by composition studies in 1989 at the Music Division of the Akademia e arteve (now University of the Arts) in Tirana. At that time, the Akademia (founded in 1962) was under heavy Soviet influence as many young Albanian composers, performers, and artists began their return home after extensive periods of study in the Soviet Union, Bulgaria, Romania, Hungary, Poland, Czechoslovakia, and the German Democratic Republic (GDR). In Albania, though, politically dissenting composers and intellectuals belonging to older generations suffered greatly under the Communist regime and, in the best of cases, had no alternative but to seek exile. The stories of Lec Kurti (1884–1948), Thoma Nassi (1892–1964), Martin Gjoka (1890–1940), Fan S. Noli (1882–1965), Murat Shehu (1897–1978), and Mikel Koliqi (1902–1997) are filled with anguish and nostalgia. The distinguished Albanian conductor and writer Eno Koço, an immigrant to the United Kingdom, sang their praises on more than one occasion.[3]

In the mid-1980s, Albanian music culture experienced a period of transition from Soviet influence to a stricter brand of Chinese Communism. Then, the fall of the Berlin Wall on November 9, 1989, rekindled hopes for most Albanians that their country would end its isolationist policies. Musicians in Albania and other countries of eastern Europe began to make contact with people in Western countries, especially in Italy, whose radio and television broadcasting stations were within the easy reach of eager Albanian listeners and viewers.

Shkurtaj's formation was initially influenced by the music of Dimitri Shostakovich, a composer much heralded during the Albanian Soviet period. However, Shostakovich's music was frowned upon when the Chinese took over the ideological and cultural indoctrination of the nation. At the same time, the music of Bela Bartók remained a constant in Shkurtaj's upbringing; it blended well with Albanian and Balkan folklore, variously jazz-influenced idioms, and virtuoso accordion playing.

The Balkan War of 1991–2001, the death of the Albanian dictator Enver Hoxha, in 1985, and the would be-appeasing government that succeeded him catapulted the country into a financial nightmare of historical proportions, triggering unprecedented "Out-of-Albania" migratory waves toward Greece on the inland and Italy across the Adriatic Sea.[4] Such migratory patterns set off a media frenzy; they were spectacles of cinematic dimensions viewed, in real time, by millions of people transfixed to their television screens across Europe and beyond. Riding that migratory wave, Admir Shkurtaj and his brother left Tirana's port city of Durrës in March 1991, determined to reach Brindisi, in the Salento subregion of Apulia.

Over the centuries, Apulia (Puglia) sacrificed millions of natives at the altar of emigration. Multitudes packed their belongings and moved north to Milan and Turin to join the work forces of the major industrialized Italian cities or went on to western Central Europe, the British Islands, the Americas, Australia, and New Zealand. They rhapsodized wholeheartedly about hope for a better life and nostalgia for their land, the ancient, dramatically labeled *finis terrae*.[5]

The Balkan War of the 1990s, though, generated a reversal of history; young Albanians viewed Apulia, and indeed the whole of Italy, as the new America, the elusive land of immigration, unrestrained consumerism, and the easy life so blatantly portrayed by the media.[6] However, the other side of that flashy coin hid horrendous stories of human trafficking across the waters of the Adriatic, contraband, drugs, prostitution, government corruption on both sides, and plenty of political missteps that fed the insidious paranoia and fear of the "other" that penetrated the psyche of many Apulian people, who generally felt the immigrants' pains and wanted to be hospitable. Some newly arrived Albanians became indeed part of local society, intermarried, had their children attend public schools, and shared their culture and music, which enriched the repertoire of many folk groups. Examples of such fusion are often showcased at the annual Notte della Taranta, a summer music/dance festival of Salento that celebrates, Woodstock-style, the local myth of the bite of the tarantula and the consequent hypnotic dance, the *pizzica*, and its variants.[7]

Following his arrival in Brindisi, Admir Shkurtaj moved to Lecce, where he enrolled at the Conservatorio "Tito Schipa," graduating in Composition in 1999. Thereafter, he pursued further studies with Sandro Gorli, Alessandro Solbiati, and Massimo Gianfreda.

Shkurtaj's compositional style is partly conditioned by his gifts as an accordion and piano virtuoso and his passion for blending free jazz and strongly colored Balkan ethnic music, neo-tarantismo modalities, and ever-expanding Mediterranean musical expressions. His recorded collections *Mesimér*, *Feksìn*, and *Gestures and Zoom* bear testimony to this eclectic blend.[8] On the academic spectrum, Shkurtaj pays homage to stylistic trends hailing from the Darmstadt avant-garde schools of the 1950s and 1960s to the catalytic works of Luciano Berio, Bruno Maderna, the microtonalists, and a host of spectral composers. However, he is very skilled at further exploring new territories by pushing to extremes instrumental and vocal extended techniques imbued with idiosyncratic serialism. *Quartetto per archi no. 2* (2008–2009) and *Katër i Radës, il naufragio*, which was awarded first prize at the 2016 Prince Pierre de Monaco Competition, are Shkurtaj's most representative academic works to date. Regarding future major undertakings, Shkurtaj is thinking about an opera centered around the figure of the Albanian dictator Enver Hoxha. The composer, his Italian wife, and their two children make their home in Lecce.

Good Friday—March 28, 1997: The Day
Tragedy Struck in the Strait of Otranto

Over the centuries, Otranto, a beautifully sunlit fortified city on the southern Adriatic coast of Salento, was the theater for many tragic events and calamities. The Ottoman invasion of 1480 remains to this day a vivid part of the city's history as the skulls of 800 citizens, beheaded for their refusal to convert to Islam, are on display in the Cattedrale di Santa Maria Annunziata. In 1534, Otranto was relentlessly under the predatory assaults of Barbary pirates springing from the Albanian coast. They committed some of the most unspeakable atrocities in the history of maritime piracy. Also, the Napoleonic Wars of 1804 inflicted much suffering on Otranto and its inhabitants, anticipating by more than a century the hecatombs caused by the World Wars of 1915–1918 and 1942–1945 as military strategists used the Strait of Otranto as a stronghold for choking any form of communication and transportation along the Adriatic corridor. Since the breakout of the Balkan conflict in 1991, hundreds of migrants have lost their lives at sea in their attempts to cross the Strait of Otranto.

Alessandro Leogrande, a relentless, passionate critic and historian of migratory patterns in the Mediterranean basin, wrote *La frontiera*, a scorching book based on migrants' stories and their crossing of the waters from Africa to Sicily in search of a future. For many, the ordeal turned into a death trap by drowning. Leogrande's chronicling gave a powerful voice to those who survived, while the expressions on the disfigured faces of those laid on the ground for identification told volumes about their suffering.[9] Another book by Leogrande, *Il naufragio: Morte nel Mediterraneo*, was dedicated to the sinking of the *Katër i Radës*.[10] There, the author reported a step-by-step account of the tragic voyage and the ensuing judiciary process related to the March 28, 1997, "accident" as it emerged from the reading and interpretation of naval codes, rules of engagement, harassment, orders, counterorders, and military interventions and the apparent suppression of evidence that evoked the slaughter of 81 Albanian men, women, and children.

The *Katër i Radës*, a Russian-built, decommissioned military patrol boat unfit to navigate the open sea but relegated to services within the Bay of Vlöra, was 70.53 feet long and 11.50 feet wide and weighed 56 tons. It could accommodate a crew of nine, at most. On that fatal Good Friday, the *Katër i Radës* sailed out of the port of Vlöra, with 122 desperate people determined to reach the port of Brindisi in Italy on board. A "crew" of three—the helmsman, a machinist, and a human trafficker—assured the crowd that the old vessel, although dangerously overloaded, would overcome the 56-mile crossing and that Brindisi would be within reach at dawn the next morning. The vessel had barely exited the Bay of Vlöra past the island of Sazan when it was intercepted by the Italian Navy frigate *Zeffiro*. The commander immediately alerted the Italian patrolling authorities that an intruding vessel loaded with "people carrying illegal arms" was on its way to the Apulian coast.[11]

The Italian Navy military corvette *Sibilla*, 285 feet long and weighing 1,265 tons, was then dispatched to stop the Albanian vessel, issuing peremptory orders to reverse course and return to its port of origin. A series of ill-advised harassment maneuvers ranging from stern warnings—met with reckless disobedience—and menacing signals followed by contradictory orders led to the fatal collision that caused the sinking of the Albanian boat and the drowning of 81 men, women, and children. The ensuing legal proceedings, initiated by victims' relatives and the catastrophe's survivors, against the *Sibilla*'s commander and the Italian Navy, resulted in an exceedingly slow-moving case that dragged from court to court, including the European Court of Human Rights, for six years before a verdict was reached and then went on for another four years as the Appellate Court of Lecce reviewed it. The case was officially closed and archived by the Supreme Court in Brindisi in May 2014. In the end, the captain of the *Sibilla* and the helmsman of the *Katër i Radës* were convicted of "shipwreck and multiple manslaughter"; the first was sentenced to three years in prison and the second to four years.

Seven months after the sinking of the *Katër i Radës*, the shipwreck, with 52 bodies still trapped inside its lower deck, was recovered from the bottom of the sea about 15 miles from Vlöra. Hauled to Brindisi, the rusty wreck lay in a fenced yard for 10 years. The bodies of the dead were identified, their names made public, and the remains returned to their families in Vlöra for proper mourning and burying. The historian Eckehard Pistrick wrote that in Vlöra:

> two symbolically charged "*lieux de mémoire*" can be identified: the sea as an abstract projection and the cemetery in Vlora where a memorial plaque was installed. The sea is the central pilgrimage where ritual acts are performed each year on the anniversary of the tragedy. Relatives of the victims walk to the shore of the Adriatic and throw bouquets of flowers into the sea. Women dressed in black share their pain and give a short statement to be broadcast on television. The almighty sea became a "*lieu de mémoire*"; one might even say a metaphoric grave that has to be honored like a physical one. Another existing *lieu de mémoire* where public commemorations of the tragedy are held is the cemetery outside

Vlora where a black marble plaque attached to two symbolic columns, called the "obelisk," was installed that bears the inscription "You went from a horror without end and you found a horrifying end." This monument is referred to in several songs.[12]

Pistrick's commentary on the tragedy's commemorations provides an in-depth analysis of a large body of commemorative songs and their variously nuanced meanings according to the interpretations of a number of Albanian artists.

The wreck of the *Katër i Radës*, stored away in Brindisi, was ultimately dismantled; the engine and parts of the wooden shell were returned to Vlöra, where the Albanian artists Arta Ngcaj, a Vlöra native, and Arben Beqiraj conceived a permanent monument as a symbol of remembrance and as a bridge for dialogue between the two sides of the Adriatic Sea. However, it appears that lack of funds prevented the realization of this project. On the other side of the Adriatic, Otranto received the hull of the vessel, which was placed on a cement platform situated in the city's large plaza before the embarcadero and the bus station—a busy place where people travel to and from land and sea. The Greek artist Costas Varotsos turned the upper half of the vessel into a superlative, evocative work of art he called *L'Approdo: Opera all'umanitá migrante sul relitto della Katër i Radës. 2012.*

Like other glass-encased pieces by Varotsos, *L'Approdo* is highly symbolic in its representation of the *Katër i Radës* submerged in crystallized water, an attempt perhaps to freeze death at a particular historical moment.

In May 2017, Admir Shkurtaj and I spent time in Otranto reflecting at the site of *L'Approdo*. Costas Varotsos's amazing artistic concept representing the ship submerged in once-crystalline, frozen water had already been severely ravaged by the fury of the sea, rain, wind, and the Salento's pounding, burning sun. The glass work, shattered to pieces, littered the rusty hull with transparent shrapnel that gave the rust the appearance of a blanket of reflecting copper dust—an unsettling image of the Adriatic forcefully reclaiming the shipwreck taken from its bottom, where it rested not in memory of the dead but as a habitat for an array of species!

Katër i Radës, il naufragio. **Opera da Camera. Musica di Admir Shkurtaj, Libretto di Alessandro Leogrande. Biennale di Venezia, 2014**

"My opera is made of water, salt and rust," says Admir Shkurtaj. A complex concept that detours a critical discourse about music and water from the time-honored Venetian *tempeste di mare* of Vivaldi and Zavateri, Wagnerian "shipwreck" dramas, and the densely realistic seascapes of Debussy and Britten to the empirical applications of "water music" of John Cage and Tan Dun, two possible forerunners of Shkurtaj's water, salt, and rust metaphor. In fact, the basic instrumental texture of this opera, consisting of some archaic elements such as the electronically altered noise of rusty pieces of metal rubbing against one another, ancient polyphonic chants sung by five male voices, the Illyrian phonology of the Albanian language, and the breathless, raspy sound of the *cupa-cupa*, give this score a uniquely southern Adriatic sound.

Beside a conductor, the score includes an ensemble of four singers: soprano, mezzo soprano, *voce popolare* ("belting" female singer), *voce sperimentale* ("shaking throat" male singer), three actors, a traditional five-male-voice iso-polyphonic ensemble, and six instrumentalists playing percussion, piano, cello, bass clarinet, trumpet and electronics, and accordion with analogue oscillators. The opera, whose duration is about 50 minutes, unfolds according to the following brief synopsis:[13]

Scene 1. Instrumental prelude consisting of four 15-minute semi-aleatoric sections.

Scene 2. Off-stage spoken monosyllabic communication between two officers of the Italian Navy on the deck of the *Zeffiro*. They review the patrolling protocol assigned to them. The instrumental ensemble underscores the dialog with a drone provided by the electronically modified accordion, joined in the last seven measures of the scene by the other four instruments.

Scene 3. The curtains lift showing Vlöra in March 1997. The city is in the midst of a full-blown civil war; shots, cries, frightening disorder, chaos, and anarchy reign supreme in the streets of a nation in disarray. The four voices on stage engage in a tour de force consisting of the hammering of rhythmic phonemes to which the instruments respond in similar fashion, imitating the onomatopoeic effects produced by the voices.

Scene 4. In this extended scene, we see people trying to flee Vlöra at all costs rushing toward the pier, where a boat is being rigged to leave for Italy. The music, frantic and electrifying, underscores the three capital tenets of this opera: civil war, escape, and the *Katër* as salvation. The dialect of the southwest region of Albania is spoken. The words' inflections, typical of that dialect, are employed as sounds, thus forming the basis of the melodic texture; the vocal quartet on stage repeats them in a chaotic series of calls and exhortations. They overlap, multiply, turn into a massive din of voices.

Scene 5. On the pier before the *Katër*, a human trafficker collects money before allowing passengers to board the vessel. While the vocalists argue with the trafficker about money, the instrumental ensemble produces a somber, sparser sound web, a premonition perhaps that the people are actually negotiating the price of their death.

Scene 6. Those able to pay begin to board the vessel. Again, this choral episode reflects sadness and hope, feelings that the composer stresses through the use of long, sustained eerie sounds.

Scene 7. As in Scene 2, offstage spoken telegraphic communication takes place between officers of the Italian Navy aboard the *Zeffiro* and the *Sibilla* discussing procedures related to the March 1997 decree that authorized all Italian patrol vessels to impede Albanian citizens fleeing the civil war to reach the coasts of Apulia. The dialog is supported by a drone provided by the electronically modified accordion.

Scene 8. The journey begins. This scene is divided in three parts: (I) The people on deck muse about the gests of Pyrrhus of Epirus, their "Italian dream" born out of the television screens, the love of music and jazz in particular. These reflections, sung in turn by solo singers, showcase vocal techniques used in Albanian polyphonic songs, rhythmic formulas derived from uneven beats and harmonic material of traditional derivation albeit electronically filtered and transformed. (II) Ermal, the male protagonist, singing with the traditional Albanian "throat trembling" voice, takes front stage and sings in Italian a very poignant "aria" followed by (III) a "choral" episode consisting of a jazz number of singular power, a clear homage to scenes from Berg's *Wozzeck* (1925) and Luciano Berio's pathbreaking *Sinfonia* (1968).

Scene 9. Again, off stage spoken telegraphic communication occurs between two officers of the Italian Navy, supported by a drone provided by the electronically modified accordion.

Scene 10. The excitement expressed in Part III of Scene 8 is suddenly disrupted by the maneuvers of harassment enacted by the *Sibilla*. Hope changes to panic, and desperation gives way to a highly melodramatic episode.

Scene 11. As the Italian military shout "*Tornate indietro!*" [Turn around—go back home), the Albanian boat people reply, "*Non abbiamo armi, solo bambini!*" [We hide no arms, just our children!]. This is the climactic moment of the opera, when the military authorities on the *Sibilla* order the herdsman of the *Katër* to return its human cargo to Albania; thus the order *Tornate indietro!* (Turn back!) However, the boat people plead with the military, saying that they conceal no arms, just their children.

The growing tension of the chorus culminates in the collision between the *Sibilla* and the *Katër*, resulting in the sinking of the small Albanian vessel.

Scene 12. In the aftermath of the tragedy, Ermal laments as he contemplates the floating dead bodies while looking for survivors. This episode runs concurrently with the following scene.

Scene 13. The officers aboard the *Sibilla* communicate to their superiors that the mission has been accomplished. A powerful juxtaposition of intents and emotions is powerfully set to music by the composer, who at this point appears to have embodied the character of Ermal on stage insomuch as he is also the instrumental ensemble's accordion player.

Scene 14. Chorus of the dead While Ermal/Admir expresses the people's collective pain over the tragedy and the vanishing of their "Italian dream," the chorus of the victims alludes to the movement of the lifeless bodies floating in the water and gives way to the final song, performed by the traditional iso-polyphonic male group as if it were in a Greek tragedy.

A Concluding Thought

Funeral gondolas continue to move gently over the Venetian Laguna and along the Canal Grande on their way to the cemetery on the island of San Michele. Franz Liszt's tragic undulating chords can still be heard in the somber surroundings. In Otranto, though, the hull of the *Katër i Radës*, molded onto a platform of cement, sheds tears made of rust and glassy dust. No sounds are heard but the growling of the wind and the sea. Death has remained frozen in time inside that hull. Admir and I, two immigrant musicians who departed from different shores and landed on others, were the only two persons observing the monument by the sea that May evening. We peered down the portholes of the hull and felt a shudder pass through our spines. *E' passata la morte* (death has passed by), we say in Salento when that happens!

Notes

1. Alan Walker, *Franz Liszt: The Final Years, 1861–1886* (Ithaca, NY: Cornell University Press, 1997), 424–425.
2. Franz Liszt was particularly fond of *La lugubre gondola*. In fact, he wrote four different versions of the piece, including one for violin (or cello) and piano. See Rossana Dalmonte, "Reflections on *La lugubre gondola*," in *Liszt and the Death of the Old Europe: Music as a Mirror of Religious, Political, Cultural, and Aesthetic Transformations*, edited by Michael Saffle and Rossana Dalmonte (Hillsdale, NY: Pendragon Press, 2003), 301–321 (Analecta Lisztiana III. Franz Liszt Studies No. 9).
3. Eno Koço, "Shostakovich, Kadaré and the Nature of Dissidence: An Albanian View," *Musical Times* 146/1890 (Spring 2005), 58–74.

4. The collapse of a financial pyramid scheme enacted by the Albanian govern- ment generated unprecedented economic, political, and social consequences. In fact, the nominal value of the pyramid schemes' liabilities amounted to almost half of the country's GDP. Most Albanians had invested in them; therefore, when the schemes collapsed, there was uncontained rioting, the government fell, and the country descended into anarchy at the brink of civil war. Some 2,000 people were killed.

5. Apulians have special feelings for their *Finis Terrae* (End of the Earth) at Santa Maria di Leuca, a strip of rocky land protruding into the Adriatic and Ionian Seas that leads the way to the Ionian Islands and their Homeric mythologies.

6. *Lamerica*, a 1994 film directed by Gianni Amelio, was based on the assumption that young Albanians regarded Italy as the America of their generation.

7. *La Notte della Taranta,* a festival taking place around the middle of August, attracts some 100,000 attendees to the town of Melpignano. Various editions of *La Notte della Taranta* have been well documented in videos and specialized publications.

8. *Mesimér* (piano solo) (Otranto: Anima Mundi Edizioni, 2011). *Gestures and Zoom* (Trio) (Abington, UK: Slam, 2012). *Feksín* (piano solo) (Otranto: Anima Mundi Edizioni, 2014).

9. Alessandro Leogrande, *Il naufragio: Morte nel Mediterraneo* (Milano: Giangi- acomo Feltrinelli, 2011).

10. Alessandro Leogrande, *La Frontiera* (Milano: Giangiacomo Feltrinelli, 2015).

11. The Italian military strategy "Operation White Flags" was established in 1997 only three days before the Otranto tragedy occurred. It functioned in effect as a naval blockade.

12. Eckehard Pistrick, *Performing Nostalgia: Migration Culture and Creativity in South Albania* (Farnham, Surrey: Ashgate, 2015), 206–207.

13. This synopsis of the opera is based on the 2014 live video performance produced by the Biennale di Venezia (www.youtube.com/watch?v=ORu3WD9lghg) and the audio recording issued by Anima Mundi in 2015.

References

Leogrande, Alessandro. *Il naufragio: Morte nel Mediterraneo*. Milano: Giangia- como Feltrinelli, 2011.

———. *La Frontiera*. Milano: Giangiacomo Feltrinelli, 2015.

Pistrick, Eckehard. *Performing Nostalgia: Migration Culture and Creativity in South Albania*. Farnham, Surrey: Ashgate, 2015.

3 Music Migrations and Creative Assimilations

The Ionian Islands

Kostas Kardamis

The geographical and social history position of the Ionian Islands made them a privileged crossroads between the so-called East and West. Their long, almost constant Western administration, especially Venetian rule, was a major factor in fostering cultural interactions since Corfu was both the Islands' administrative center and a preeminent gateway in and out of the Adriatic Sea.[1] It is gradually becoming apparent that these factors created a receptive environment that eventually led to the amalgamation of seemingly opposite cultural realms. Undeniably, music was part of this "shared world," and, as a cultural manifestation concerning all social classes, it was particularly characterized by convergences and divergences closely related to cultural migrations that took place around the Adriatic Sea.

The year 1549 could be considered an emblematic point in this amalgamation. In that year, a contract penned in Greek was signed in Corfu between a descendant of a Peloponessian refugee family and a professional music teacher from Calabria. It regarded the teaching of the natural trumpet.[2] Nonetheless, it is well known today that at that time professional or semiprofessional musicians, as well as those conscripted in the Venetian and Dalmatian armed forces, had already participated in official state music ensembles that performed at religious and public ceremonies.[3] Moreover, a century earlier, in 1449, Zorzi Trombetta, a trumpet player born in the Peloponessian port of Modon, then under Venetian administration, had already performed during his naval service in Corfu and other Venetian-dominated cities of the Adriatic route such as Ragusa, Zara (Zadar), and Cattaro (Kotor).[4] Actually, Zorzi Trombetta da Modon became an influential figure in the formation of Venetian wind ensembles during that period. Venetian, Greek, and Dalmatian musicians were not, of course, the only performers who frequented the islands of the Ionian Sea at that time; it is indicative that in Zante in 1599, during May Day festivities, five trumpeters hailing from an English ship played the opening tune.[5] The geopolitical rivalry between Venice and the Ottoman Empire was the cause of two major sieges of Corfu,

in 1537 and 1716, during which the characteristic martial music of both
sides was heard. On the other hand, Venice's defeat in the 1716 Venetian-
Turkish War offered Antonio Vivaldi the opportunity to compose the highly
allegorical "military oratorio" *Juditha Triumphans*, in which the protagonist
is symbolically associated with the Adriatic Sea and Venice. Corfu's popular
music was also known among the eighteenth-century Venetians; even Carlo
Goldoni made particular reference to the "canzonette di Corfu."[6]

Moreover, the polyphonic nature of the Ionian Orthodox chant was
known to Gioseffo Zarlino, and its use in the Greek church of Venice was
emphatically reported by Charles Burney two centuries later.[7] The polyphonic texture of Ionian Orthodox sacred music is related to the four-part
improvisatory polyphony that used to characterize the music of rural areas
(to be discussed later), where the highest voice is leading and the rest follow by adding appropriate intervals.[8] This practice in Orthodox chanting,
called "Cretan Chant" (because of its supposed relation to similar practices
that were imported to the Ionian Islands by Cretan refugees), can be traced
at least to the sixteenth century and spread over the subsequent years. An
interesting parallel exists also in the music of Corfu's Jewish community.
The musical practice of the Sephardites was called "bel canto" or "idioma
pugliese," since it was supposed to have come from the Puglia region in
southern Italy and thus was different from that practiced by Corfu's Jewish people.[9] If one adds to these elements the music of Roman Catholic
churches, which followed the practices dictated by Rome, it becomes obvious that the various religious groups of the Islands offered an additional
musical mosaic, which, among others, caught indigenous composers' attention during the nineteenth century regardless of the rite they followed.

These are only selective instances demonstrating that the Adriatic Sea
was a particularly active musical route long before the nineteenth century,
when this reciprocal engagement reached its peak.

Nineteenth Century: Culmination of the Creative Assimilation

As expected, opera played a decisive role in spreading art music and in its
creative assimilation by Ionian audiences. The earliest opera performance
was in Corfu in 1733 at the Nobile Teatro di San Giacomo. The event ignited
the development of a vivid musical culture in the region and the larger
nineteenth-century art music paradigm in Greece.

In this respect, reciprocal migrations of both cultural manifestations
and artists had a pivotal effect. Italian music and melodrama played the
role of a musical "lingua franca" in the Ionian Islands, as in the rest of
Europe. As early as the eighteenth century, then, a common aesthetic and

musical matrix for the urban societies and the emerging Ionian composers was formed. Nonetheless, operatic performances on an organized annual basis did not seem to take place in Corfu between 1733 and 1771,[10] but this period has not yet been thoroughly researched.[11] In any case, between 1771 and the mid-1930s, Corfu witnessed incessant operatic activity, even in times of war.[12]

The popularity of opera among the Corfiots, in combination with the melodrama's central position in European art and society, led to its dissemination to the other Ionian Islands during the course of the nineteenth century. The earliest opera performances in Zante and Cephalonia took place in 1813[13] and 1836,[14] respectively. Permanent operatic theaters were also erected on these islands during the nineteenth century.

The development of the operatic repertoire in Corfu during the eighteenth and on the other Ionian Islands during the nineteenth century followed that of Italian theaters of their respective times, facilitating the connections between cultures. The same theaters served also as local concert halls, where recitals and instrumental concerts by local amateurs, traveling virtuosos, and theater orchestras took place. Nevertheless, even in these cases, opera always had a dominant place in the repertoires.

There is no need here to emphasize that the marine routes of the Adriatic played a vital role in the establishment and maintenance of these dynamics. Opera companies usually gathered in Ancona or Otranto prior to traveling to the Ionian Islands, following their scheduled itineraries. Italian impresarios were the forces behind this operatic activity, but there were also instances when Ionians participated in or even assumed full responsibility for the operatic season, thus revealing the reciprocal connection inspired by this cultural migration.[15] Moreover, several musicians and singers from Marche, Puglia, and Abruzzo regions of Italy found permanent or semipermanent engagements in the Ionian theaters.[16] The place of the eastern Adriatic coast should also be emphasized; the Battagel family, which came from Gorizia (in today's Slovenia) and was active in Zara, moved permanently in 1800 to Corfu, where the family played an important role in opera productions and concert activities. In 1800, they also were the charter members of a proposal outlining the "impresa" of the Corfu's theater, clearly illustrating the cultural amalgamation of the Adriatic music migrations within the common operatic realm. This "compania d'impresa" consisted of Giovanni and Francesco Battagel of Gorizia, "maestro concertatore" Stefano Moretti from Marche, the musicians and teachers Girolamo and Stefano Pojago (second-generation immigrants from Milan living permanently in Corfu), and four local citizens.[17] The Adriatic routes were also a vital section of the Levantine operatic network, which extended from Patras, Athens, Malta, and Alexandria to Syros, Smyrna, and Constantinople.

As far as musical instruction was concerned, it is clear now that musical education was present in Corfu long before the emergence of opera performances and that beginning in the sixteenth century the teaching of music was entrusted to private tutors. However, from late in the eighteenth century, the musical performance among the wealthy Ionian classes was a distinctive element, and the emergence of operatic activity further supported that interest. Musicians (initially of Italian origin) who were directly or indirectly associated with the various theatrical productions of the Ionian Islands and lived there on a permanent or semipermanent basis also offered private lessons. On the other hand, professional music teaching was usually connected with a sort of underground league of local musicians insomuch as any professional connection with music was not considered socially proper by the local wealthy classes.

Music lessons were included in the curricula of both public and private girls' schools as early as the 1820s[18] only as optional instruction, since the activity of the private teachers in their own domiciles could not be neglected. The 1841 educational statute included music, again, as an option in boys' schools exclusively within the curriculum of the Ionian College.[19] In both cases, music lessons do not seem to have exceeded the limits allowed for a well-cultivated bourgeois dilettante and seen as most desirable for a daughter and future wife.

Between 1824 and 1828, musical instruction was included within the curriculum of the Ionian Academy, where the teaching of Orthodox chant and the rudiments of "Western" secular music were strongly supported by Lord Guilford, the Academy's founder and rector.[20] Before that, Guilford had sponsored the training in secular music of the deacon Ioannis Aristeidis from Ioannina, who studied in Naples between 1819 and 1824.

The gradual change of local conditions, combined with the presence of a group of locally based tutors, led Ionians to adopt the models of the Italian musical education system for professional and semiprofessional training. In this respect, the creation of local philharmonic institutions was important. These music schools were both educational institutions (for their students) and concert clubs (for their subscribers). Moreover, the fact that people from all social classes could attend their educational activities contributed to the dissemination of musical instruction among formerly excluded social strata. Their activities also underlined the cultural dynamic of the migration of culture and people to and from that area of the Adriatic Sea.

The earliest, albeit short-lived, Ionian philharmonic institution was founded in Zante in 1816[21] under the directorship of Marco Battagel, a descendant of the family mentioned earlier. Similar societies were established in Cephalonia (1836, 1837) and, later, in Lefkada (1850), all of which focused their efforts on forming civic wind ensembles.[22] However, the premiere Ionian music institution was the Corfu Philharmonic Society, founded in 1840, which established its wider educational aims at its founding. Its initial founders openly expressed their wish to create a musical establishment based on European prototypes that could eventually evolve into a musical academy.

Consequently, the Corfu Philharmonic Society differed from similar organizations established on the other Ionian Islands, which focused almost exclusively on maintaining wind ensembles. The students of the Corfu Philharmonic Society were taught piano and various string, woodwind, and brass instruments. Moreover, lessons included vocal music, choral singing, and theoretical subjects such as harmony, orchestration, counterpoint, and composition. The activities of the Corfu Philharmonic Society contributed to the emergence of Greek performers, teachers, and composers, who from the mid-nineteenth century assumed a central role in the musical life of the Ionian Islands and mainland Greece, often succeeding their Italian colleagues.

The vivid social environment of Corfu, which was closely associated with the Adriatic routes, was reflected also in the students of its Philharmonic Society; besides the Greek, the Maltese, and the Italian students (some of them from families that had been living in Corfu for generations), there were students whose ancestors had migrated to the island by following the eastern Adriatic coast. For instance, the ophicleide player Filippos Devaris, whose father was born in Trieste and whose mother was born in today's Croatia, was one of the Philharmonic's earliest bandsmen and from the late 1840s a member of both the Corfu theater's orchestra and the British fleet wind band; the horn player Georgios Georgovich also played in Corfu's theater and later taught in the band of the Syros School for Destitute Children; Leonidas Rafaelovich, whose family came to Corfu from Cattaro in the mid-eighteenth century, belonged to the Corfu theater's personnel. Later he became a distinguished military bandmaster and the music director of the Mantzaros Philharmonic Society, founded in Corfu in 1890.

Beginning in the late nineteenth century, civic bands also sprang up in rural areas of the Ionian Islands. It is particularly important to note that the musical conditions in the Ionian urban centers facilitated the musical activities of the middle class and the "lower orders." It comes as no surprise that the civic bands, choral ensembles, and, later, the mandolinatas (mandolin orchestras) became the main tools for the "popularization" of art music's achievements among wider social strata through repertoires that, directly or not, reflected the cultural dynamic of this "shared world." The same applied to a large part of their audiences. The continuous contact of the lower classes with wind ensembles, initially during the course of religious ceremonies or festivals, led to the bands' increasing popularity among the members of social groups the majority of which had no access to opera performances or private musical events.

If nothing else, military wind bands were a constant presence on the Islands beginning in the early Venetian era, making them the music ensembles with the longest continuous activity in the region and, at the same time, a familiar musical manifestation for the Ionian Islands' urban and semi-urban societies. As has already been remarked, these ensembles brought to the Ionian Islands several musicians from Italy, France, Germany, and the eastern Adriatic coast, adding some interesting aspects to music migrations that combined common cultural experience with the musicians' personal endeavors. Indicative of such migrations was the fact that Hyacinthe Eléonore Klosé, the person responsible for modern clarinet technique, was born in 1808 in Corfu, where his father, Joseph Klosé, was serving as military musician while performing also in the "Column of Harmony" of the Saint Napoleon Military Masonic Lodge.[23] During the British administration, the bands of the British regiments stationed on the Islands included many Italian musicians and, after the 1840s, also students from the Philharmonic Society.[24] In this way, the Adriatic cultural routes became largely responsible for the formation of military bands consisting of European instrumentalists, even on the Ottoman-occupied mainland at the service of Ali Pasha.[25] On the other hand, a century later, such was the dissemination and the popularity of the civic bands in the region that the Banda Comunale of Galatina (Province of Lecce) considered it necessary to pay a visit to Corfu's philharmonic institutions on its return home after having participated in the 1906 Athens Inter-Olympiad.[26]

The impact of the various, mainly male, choral societies (despite not being organized according to the practices of the choral societies of the wider region or the French *orphéon* societies), as well as of the mandolinatas, was analogous to that of the wind ensembles. Choral singing, known in the Ionian Islands for its traditional improvisatory polyphony, was gradually enriched with elements derived from "learned" practices, was systematized through the establishment of choral schools, and became a creative factor in the creation of a rich urban repertoire. This contributed considerably to the social expansion of Greek poetry and facilitated close contacts with literature and music among all social classes, both within and outside the regional limits of the Ionian Islands.

Indigenous Composers

The conditions outlined so far contributed to the emergence of indigenous composers, whose creativity captured these dynamic cultural migrations while supporting the demand for "national music" during the nineteenth and

twentieth centuries.[27] Most of them created works that belonged to the operatic genre, and all of them contributed to establishing the Ionian urban song,
both in Italian and particularly in Greek verses. Moreover, they contributed
to the sacred music repertoire of both Orthodox and Catholic rites and promoted concurrently an interest in instrumental music, especially after the
1860s, when some composers became actively acquainted with developments in France and Germany. At the same time, movement of people along
the Adriatic routes continued, but in this instance it was the Ionians who
migrated to the European mainland in order to enlarge their musical knowledge and gain experience and new ideas.

Nonetheless, the earliest indigenous composer, Nikolaos Halikiopoulos Mantzaros, never considered himself a professional composer.[28] His
training under the players of Corfu's San Giacomo theater, such as Stefano Pojago, had a decisive influence on his early works. If nothing else,
Pojago composed the music for the opera *Gli amanti confusi ossia il brutto
fortunato* (Corfu, 1791)[29] and for a "ballo eroico" titled *L'arrivo d'Ulisse
alla Isola de' Feaci* (Corfu, 1818)—echoing the widely spread neoclassi-
cal convictions about the island's Homeric past. Mantzaros's subsequent
teachers were also connected with the Adriatic routes; his first instructor in
counterpoint was Stefano Moretti. Mantzaros concluded his studies in 1813
with a certain "cavaliere" Barbati, possibly a Neapolitan political refugee.
Mantzaros's public debut took place in 1815 in the San Giacomo theater,
where his *Aria Greca*—the earliest composition set to Greek verses for
voice and orchestra—was also presented in 1827. It was sung by Elisabetta
Pinotti, the Italian prima donna of the company, and Marco Battagel led the
orchestra from the first violin desk. Two years later Mantzaros began work
on Solomos's *Hymn to Liberty*, the opening stanzas of which, in 1865, were
officially adopted as the Greek national anthem. Before that, between 1819
and 1826, Mantzaros used the Adriatic routes to visit the most important
musical centers of Italy, possibly at the suggestion of Giuseppe Castignace,
the Neapolitan "maestro concertatore" of Corfu's theater. During his time
in Naples he became a close associate and friend of Niccolò Zingarelli and
a fervent supporter of Neapolitan educational methods. It is of particular
importance that in the 1830s Mantzaros was considered the characteristic
representative of the classic Neapolitan style,[30] revealing today a previously
neglected aspect of these mutual cultural migrations.

Concurrent to this, a rather obscure and not yet fully documented aspect
of these Adriatic connections regarding music theory concerns a certain
"Spiridione Pascquicoli" from Corfu, who in 1811 studied with the famous
Stanislao Mattei in Bologna.[31]

Mantzaros's students Antonios Liberalis (1814–1842) and Iossif Liberalis (1819–1899) had since the late 1830s been helping to meet the demand

for national music.[32] The brothers were the sons of the military bandmaster Domenico Liberali, from Fermo (a city near Ancona), and his Greek wife, from Zante, proving the multiplicity of the Adriatic migrations' outcomes.

The liberal movements that characterized this period contributed to another aspect of the musical connections related to the Adriatic. Among the numerous exiles who found refuge in the Ionian Islands were several men of letters, who brought with them both patriotic ideas and achievements in their respective fields. For example, Paolo Costa (1771–1836) and Niccoló Tommaseo (1802–1874), two leading figures of the Italian Risorgimento, offered to Corfu both their philosophical thoughts and their poetic skills, which became the creative basis for some popular songs by Mantzaros. Tommaseo in particular became a rather emblematic figure in these forced Adriatic migrations. Born in Sebenico (in today's Croatia), he demonstrated active interest in Italian culture without neglecting that of his native region; he became a fervent supporter of the Italian struggle and elected Corfu as his place of exile. He remained on the island for a number of years.

More local composers, most of them Mantzaros's students, appeared during the 1840s. These included Domenikos Padovas (1817–1892), who, on February 1857, presented in Corfu his opera *Dirce*, based on a libretto by the Italian political exile Severiano Fogacci, from Ancona.[33] Furthermore, Padovas composed one-movement instrumental overtures as early as 1830. In 1855, Spyridon Xyndas (1817–1896) presented in the San Giacomo theater his opera *Anna Winter*, based on Dumas's *Les Trois Mousquetaires*. This work is the earliest operatic adaptation of Dumas's celebrated work and became the first of a series of operas by the same composer, which further expanded his fame, gained initially through his songs in Greek. Xyndas's most widely known opera was *The Parliamentary Candidate* (premiered in Corfu in 1867), the first full-scale operatic work in Greek, which constituted a milestone in the quest for "Greek national music." That is because it used Greek vernacular language in its libretto and extensive folk musical elements, mostly derived from Ionian Islands, as basic structural parts of its music. At the same time, this opera was a critique against then-current political morals.

Pavlos Karrer (1829–1896), from Zante, was the first Ionian composer to achieve considerable success among Italian operatic audiences (especially in Milan) during the 1850s with the operas *Dante e Bice* (1852), *Isabella d'Aspeno* (1854), and *La rediviva* (1856). Upon his return to Greece in 1858, he also worked on melodramas inspired by the recent history of the newly established Greek Kingdom, beginning with the emblematic *Markos Botzaris*. His creative output from that point on was characterized by the coexistence of compositions meant for the Greek and the international audience.[34]

Spyridon Samáras (1861–1917), a descendant of a merchant family from Siatista (Macedonia), whose Vienna-born father was appointed in 1858 to the Greek Consulate in Corfu, studied in Athens and France but made his career in Italy.[35] There he became famous for the operas *Flora mirabilis* (1886), *Lionella* (1891), *La martire* (1894), *Storia d'amore* (1903), *Mademoiselle de Belle Isle* (1907), and *Rhea* (1908), long before (and long after) the composition of the *Olympic Anthem* (Athens, 1896), which eventually secured him posthumous fame. Born in Cephalonia, Dionysios Lavrangas (1860–1941) was trained in Naples and France and became known for his operatic and orchestral music, as well as for his efforts to disseminate opera among Greek audiences through the activities of the Greek Opera Company. The musical production of the Lambelet family (whose Swiss-born patriarch reached Corfu after a successful career in Naples) was also centered, though not exclusively, on musical theater. Napoleon Lambelet (1864–1932), also trained in Naples, was successful in London's musical theaters during the early twentieth century. He contributed to the fin-de-siècle song in Greek during his stay in Athens.

Dionysios Rodotheatos (1849–1892), educated in Corfu, Naples, and Milan, was considered the "foremost Wagnerite" of his generation. Besides operas, his work included symphonic works.[36] Several other composers who were active well into the twentieth century could be added here if space permitted. All these composers helped meet the demand for "Greek national music," a quest dating from the late eighteenth century, initially through compositions in the Greek language and gradually through patriotic operatic plots and the use of folklore elements.[37]

The activities of women composers are an aspect of the Ionian Islands' music not widely acknowledged until recently. Their compositions ranged from popular piano or vocal works related to their conventional participation in the domestic entertainment, especially during the nineteenth century, to the works of the highly educated Eleni Lambiri (1888–1960) and the modernist Alexandra Lekka-Sakali (1917–2012). The Adriatic routes were also evident in the case of Francesca Coraggiou. She composed a prize-winning polka in 1875 and was the granddaughter of a Sicilian merchant who had emigrated to Corfu during the Napoleonic period. Similarly, Parthenope Barker, whose works were published with distinction during the late nineteenth century, was the daughter of a British merchant, banker, and vice consul of Sweden to Corfu.[38] Both of them were Xyndas's students and opera devotees.

This brief reference to women who contributed to music in the Ionian Islands offers the opportunity to remark on two Ionian opera singers who were typical products of the region's nineteenth-century cultural and physical migrations. Elena d'Angri (1821–1886) was the daughter of a Neapolitan immigrant, who came to Corfu during the Napoleonic wars. After initial studies in her hometown, Elena moved to Naples and Florence under her uncle's protection. Her debut in Lucca in 1843 launched an international career, which brought her to Austria, Russia, France, Britain, Spain, and North America.[39] The Zante-born Isavella Yatrá (c.1838–1916) was English (on her mother's side) and studied in Bologna but returned to Zante, where, until 1864, she played the protagonist in several operas. In 1859, she married Pavlos Karrer.[40]

Of particular importance was the Ionians' little-known pursuit of musical aesthetics beginning in the eighteenth century. The range of their contributions was indicative of the different periods in which they were written and reflected the ideas that affected their authors.[41] Regarding the issue of national music, it was of particular importance that the earliest manifesto on music nationalism in Greece was written in 1901 by Georgios Lambelet (1875–1945), a descendant of this musical family. It is also interesting to observe here that the earliest treatise by a Greek about what is today called music therapy was published in 1787 in Venice under the title *Della forza della Musica nelle passioni, nei costumi e dell'uso medico del ballo*. The author of this medical and aesthetic treatise was Ioannis Fragkiskos Tzoulatis (1762–1805), a doctor from Cephalonia and a devoted operagoer in Corfu. His ideas about musical theater were evident in his work.

Music of Rural Areas

The musical features found in Ionian rural areas may be classified among those of the Northeastern Mediterranean group. Nonurban vocal practice, as it is preserved in Zante, Cephalonia, and some Corfiot villages, is characterized by a type of improvisatory polyphony that is comparable to similar Adriatic and wider Mediterranean traditions.[42] This musical genre is known as "arekia," from the Italian phrase "a orecchio," meaning "by ear."[43] It is a four-part improvisatory polyphonic genre, where the highest voice leads. As it has already been pointed out, similar practices were also adopted in the performance of the liturgical chant of the Orthodox Church in the Ionian Islands.

Other rural genres, mostly monophonic and more rhythmic, involved a melodic antiphonal scheme between vocal and instrumental parts. The most common instruments in folk ensembles today are guitars and violins.[44] But, in the early twentieth century, the typical rural ensemble was "tambourloniakaro," a rather common ensemble in the greater region, which consisted of a drum and a double-reed wind instrument. Supposedly imported from the mainland,[45] apart from its use for the entertainment of the peasantry from the fifteenth century, "tambourloniakaro" was a particular sonic emblematic ensemble of the gypsies living in Corfu and was later the musical emblem for the official reviews of the peasants' militia forces.[46] It comes as no surprise that, in 1867, Xyndas extesively used "tambourloniakaro" in his opera *The Parliamentary Candidate* not only in terms of melodic motives related to the peasantry of Corfu but also through its actual timbral texture (performed by an oboe and timpani), thus adding realism to the opera, which takes place in a Corfiot village.

Turbulent Times

The twentieth century brought to the Ionian Islands two world wars and some not so widely known musical aspects related to migration along the Adriatic corridor. It is said that the origin of World War I may have been etched at the summer residence of German Kaiser Wilhelm in Corfu. This remains to be confirmed, but it is beyond doubt that the Kaiser left to Corfu a dance that is still considered by many to be an original rural dance. Parallel to this, the Kaiser's numerous visits to Corfu played a decisive role in the commissioning of the opera *Kerkyra* (1912),[47] in which the ancient past met the picturesque and imagined folklore and fin-de-siècle convictions about ancient Greek music combined with folkloric tunes. On the other hand, the operetta *The Princess of Sasson* by Samáras (premiered in Athens in February 1915) used the idealized scenery of the Adriatic coast to demonstrate in a comic, albeit sincere way at the beginning of World War I the geopolitical struggles that had already created conflict in the larger area.

World War I and Greece's later alliance with the Entente transformed Corfu into a military base, thus beginning a rather truculent period with regard to its Adriatic connections. It was in Corfu that the remains of the Serbian army and government found refuge and regrouped in 1916. It was also there that the initial agreement toward the creation of the Kingdom of Yugoslavia was signed on June 30, 1917. As during every war, music played a major role both in propaganda and in uplifting the people's morale. These facts add some musical aspects of this violent Adriatic migration that are worth mentioning.

The theater in Corfu was the site of opera performances by Italian companies on a regular basis during the war, presenting the standard Italian opera repertoire and continuing in this way the conventional Adriatic cultural routes.[48] At the same time, it is indicative that the emblematic Serbian national song *Tamo daleko* [There, far away] was composed in Corfu at this time, and it is still performed today on the occasion of the Serbians' annual visit to the island for the commemoration of their ancestors' dislocation. This is something to be expected, since already during the war period Serbian and Greek artists joined forces by performing songs in their respective languages in order to strengthen the people's morale.[49]

The mingling of musical cultures during the same period was made particularly obvious through the most ubiquitous of music ensembles during times of conflict, namely the military band. The bands of the French Zouaves,[50] the Allied Fleet,[51] the joined bands of the Slovenian and Serbian army, the Italian army,[52] or the military forces' combined bands[53] offered nearly every day a different musical background and a series of weekly concerts, which were added to those of the already existing wind bands of the island.[54]

The activities of the Sloveno-Serbian military band are of particular importance, both because they are related to the eastern Adriatic coast and because band members were among those war refugees who endured severe losses before and during their coming to Corfu.[55] The band's concert activity is also interesting because of its repertoire, which consisted not only of opera excerpts from the standard (i.e., Italian) repertoire, marches, and widely known dance music but also of wind-band arrangements of works by composers from the greater region of the western Balkans, thus underlining the new territorial developments that led to the creation of the Kingdom of Yugoslavia. It is interesting that the repertoire of the Sloveno-Serbian band included, besides the standard works, arranged parts from the emblematic opera *Nikola Zrinjski*, by the influential composer Ivan Zajc (born in today's Croatia),[56] and dance music by Jovo Janisevich (born in today's Montenegro),[57] as well as selections of Serbian melodies and songs.[58]

Because of the forced Serbian migration, the audience of Corfu (both the indigenous music lovers and the military personnel) encountered a repertoire related to the emerging multiethnic Kingdom of Yugoslavia, the music activities of which were considered to be at the "margins" of the conventional Western music perception.[59] To this, one may add the performance of Russian songs arranged for wind band,[60] as well as a selection from Tchaikovsky's *Eugene Onegin*,[61] completing, in a sense, this rather peculiar and Corfu-related musical reference to the pan-Slavism in the Balkans and along the eastern Adriatic Coast. This is further underlined by the performance of Davorin Jenko's symphonic work *Kossovo* by an Italian military band,[62] thus featuring a work by a composer born in today's Slovenia who nonetheless, through his activities in Belgrade, became a musical herald of Serbian and pan-Slavic nationalism.

The musicians of the Sloveno-Serbian military ensembles also participated, both as wind band and as string orchestra, in the activities of Corfu's cinema.[63] The changes that came after the intervention of the United States in World War I were also reflected in the Sloveno-Serbian ensemble's repertory, since works related to the new member of the alliance were included in the band's programs.[64]

This short overview of the turbulent period during the first half of the twentieth century cannot omit a shadowy political use of the important cultural and multileveled dynamic that characterized the Ionian Islands for such a long time. Following the nineteenth century's ideas of Italian expansionism, as they were codified by the "Cavour doctrine," the Ionian Islands became part of the "vital space" of Mussolini's regime. Corfu's brief occupation in 1923 constituted an early sign of this ideology and resulted, among other things, in the suspension of Italian opera companies in Corfu's theater. This terminated a two-centuries-long practice, which was partly replaced by the activities of local musicians and of the Greek Operatic Company under Lavrangas. However, when between 1941 and 1943 the Ionian Islands were under fascist occupation, the Italian cultural connections were again particularly emphasized by propaganda. The Italian connections of some of the aforementioned Ionian composers were particularly underlined, whereas their contributions regarding Greek national music was minimalized. Parallel to this, the Italian Radio Station of Corfu broadcast opera as part of its propaganda practices, and its orchestra performed a carefully selected repertoire.[65]

The politically oriented and one-sided use of a particularly vivid cultural dynamic for nonmusical endeavors did not diminish the role of the Adriatic cultural ties to the Ionian Islands. During the postwar era, the importance of this multileveled culture persisted, even during the politically and culturally demanding periods of the 1960s, 1970s, and 1980s and despite the parallel gradual turn of the popular culture toward "orientalized stereotypes" for the sake of the tourism industry. The visits of Italian artists and Yugoslav music ensembles after 1950, as well as the international (and regrettably neglected by the Ionians) career of the modernist composer Gaetano Giuffré (born in Corfu in 1917), are just a few examples that prove that this long-honored dynamic of the Adriatic routes retained its strength.

Notes

1. The Ionian Islands, also called the Heptanese, comprise Corfu, Paxos, Lefkada, Cephalonia, Ithaca, Zante, and Cythera. After the twelfth century the islands came gradually under Frankish rule, but their social and cultural formulation was a result of the Venetian administration, which, however, did not begin at the same time in all the islands. The first of the islands to come under Venetian authority was Corfu, in 1386, and the last was Lefkada, in 1684. After the fall of the Venetian Republic (1797), the Ionian Islands were governed by the Republican French (1797–1799) before becoming an independent Greek state under Russian protection (1800–1807), thus forming the earliest independent Greek state in modern times, a Napoleonic satellite state (1807–1814), and a British protectorate (1815–1864). On June 2, 1864, the Ionian Islands were officially annexed to the Greek Kingdom.

2. The contract's text is published in Andreas Grammenos, "I moussiki stin Kerkyra: Istoria aeonon," *I Kerkyra Simera* (5 August 2009), 8. It reveals interesting parallels with the musical education in Crete at roughly the same time. See Nikolaos M. Panagiotakis, *I paedeia kai I moussiki stin Kriti kata tin Venetokratia* (Crete, 1990), 95, and "I mousiki sti venetokratoumeni Kriti," *Thysavrismata* 20 (1990), 9–169.

3. Important information covering the period between the fourteenth and eighteenth centuries can be found in Aliki Nikiforou, *Dimosies teletes stin Kerkyra kata tin periodo tis Venetikis Kyriarchias* (Athens: Themelio, 1999), 113, 172, 178, 180, 212, 240.

4. Regarding Zorzi Trombetta and his contribution, see Daniel Leech-Wilkinson, "Il libro di appunti di un suonatore di tromba del quindicesimo secolo," *Rivista Italiana di Musicologia* 16 (1981), 16–39; Rodolfo Baroncini, "Zorzi Trombetta and the Band of *Piffari* and Trombones of the *Serenissima*: New Documentary Evidence," *Historic Brass Society Journal* 14 (2002), 59–82; and Rodolfo Baroncini, "Zorzi Trombetta da Modon and the Founding of the Band of *Piffari* and *Tromboni* of the *Serenissima*," *Historic Brass Society Journal* 16 (2004), 1–18.

5. P. G. Kallinikos, "Enas Agglos sti Zakyntho to Pascha tou 1599," *Deltion Anagnostikis Etairias Kerkyras* 16 (1979), 213–218. Possibly it is worth mentioning in the broader discussion of migrations that the English ship carried a mechanical musical instrument to Constantinople as a gift from Queen Elizabeth I to the Ottoman Sultan.

6. Carlo Goldoni, *La famiglia dell'antiquario* (Monaco: Franz, 1847), 60.

7. Gioseffo Zarlino, *Le istituzioni harmoniche* (Venezia, 1558), 152, and Charles Burney, *A General History of Music from the Earliest Ages to the Present Period* (London, 1782), ii, 52.

8. This practice is described in Panagiotis Gritsanis, "Peri tis ton Ionion Nison ekklisiastikis moussikis," *Ethnikon Imerologion* 8 (1868), 325–336. See also Markos Dragoumis, "I dytikizousa ekklisiastiki moussiki mas stin Kriti kai sta Eptanisa," *Laografia* 31 (1976–1978), 272–293; Markos Dragoumis, "Prosfates erevnes sti Zakyntho gia tin ekklisiastiki mas moussiki," *Bulletin of the Ionian Academy* 2 (1986), 270–280; Markos Dragoumis, *I moussiki paradosi tis zakynthinis ekklisias* (Athens, 2000), 19; Markos Dragoumis, "I moussiki ton Ellinon: Ekklisiastiki, kosmiki, dimotiko tragoudi," in *Istoria tou Neou Ellinismou*, 10 vols. (Athens: Ellinika Grammata, *Ta Nea*, 2003), ii, 221–238: 221; Efstathios Makris, "I paradosiaki ekklisiastiki moussiki ton Eptanison: Synoliki istoriki prosegisi," *Moussikos Loghos* 8 (Winter 2009), 45–70.

9. A detailed overview is offered by Emmanouela Kavvadia in *I moussiki paradosi ton synagogon tis Kerkyras kai ton Ioanninon: Mia ethnomoussikologiki prossegisi*, bachelor's dissertation (Corfu: Ionian University Music Department, 2004).

10. Platonas Mavromoustakos, "Apo ton Arlekino ston Loengrin: To theatro San Tziakomo kai i theatriki zoe tis Kerkyras (17ᵒˢ–19ᵒˢ aeonas)," in *Kerkyra: Istoria, astiki zoe kai architektoniki 14ᵒˢ–19ᵒˢ aeonas*, edited by Ennio Concina and Aliki Nikiforou-Testone (Corfu, 1994), 71–78; Platonas Mavromoustakos, "To italiko melodrama sto theatro San Tziakomo tis Kerkyras," *Paravasis* 1 (1995), 147–191; and Platonas Mavromoustakos, "I proti parastasi italikou melodramatos sto theatro San Tziakomo tis Kerkyras (1733): Vevaiotites kai erotimata," *Porfyras* 114 (January–March 2005), 581–590.

11. For example, in 1766 a 30-year-old tenor, Francesco Piccoli, who was specializing in *opera buffa*, wrote in a letter to the legendary Padre Giovanni Battista Martini that at least three years earlier he had sung in Corfu. See John Rosselli, "From Princely Service to the Open Market: Singers of Italian Opera and Their Patrons, 1600–1850," *Cambridge Opera Journal* 1 (1989), 1–32: 31.

12. For the eighteenth century, see Mavromoustakos, "To italiko melodrama." For the nineteenth century, see Kostas Kardamis, "Nees eidiseis gia ti melodramatiki drastiriotita tou theatrou San Giacomo metaksy 1799 kai 1823" [New Information for the Operatic Activities of San Giacomo Theater between 1799 and 1823], paper delivered at the conference *Ionian Opera and Music Theatre until 1953* (Athens Megaron Concert Hall, 23–24 April 2010), published in the Proceedings of the conference, available online from the Department of Theater Studies of the Athens University (www.theatre.uoa.gr), 42–53 ; Kostas Sambanis, "Parastasiologio operon pou anavivasthikan sta theatra ton Eptanison apo italikous epaggelmatikous thiasous ton 19o aiona (1820–1900)" [Opera Performances Staged in the Ionian Islands' Theaters by Italian Professional Troupes during the 19th Century (1820–1900)], *Moussikos Ellinomnimon* 18–19 (May–December 2014), 24–41; and Giorgos Leotsakos, *Spiros Samáras* (Athens: Benaki Museum, 2013), 53–126.

13. For an overview of the operatic activity in Zante, see Nikias Lountzis, *I Zakynthos meta moussikis*, 3 vols. (Athens, 2009), ii, 224–354; Kostas Sambanis, "Oi parastaseis operas stin Zakyntho apo to 1835 eos tin ensomatosi ton Eptanison sto 'Vasileion tis Ellados,'" *Polyphonia* 21 (Fall 2012), 7–51; Kostas Sambanis, *Polyphonia* 22 (Spring 2013), 35–74. See also Stelios Tzerbinos, *I diataksiki metheksi sti latreia tis operas kai to Elliniko Melodrama sti Zakyntho* (Zante: Bastas, 1999). However, the presence of the impresario Gregorio Cicuzzi in Zante in 1783 (Lountzis, *I Zakynthos meta moussikis*, 34, 225) might suggest at least an earlier attempt to stage opera there, especially if one takes into account that Cicuzzi was going to be the impresario of the San Giacomo theater of Corfu from autumn 1784 through the Carnival 1786 season (Mavromoustakos, *I italiki opera*, 171–173).

14. Regarding the theatrical activities in Cephalonia, as well as possible earlier opera performances in the theater of Spyridon Berettas in Argostoli (1805–c1825), see Spyridon Evangelatos, *Istoria tou theatrou en Kefalinia* (Athens, 1970). A detailed account of the performances between 1837 and 1864 appears in Kostas Sambanis, "Oi parastaseis operas stin Kefalonia apo tin idrysi tou theatrou 'Solomou' eos ta prota eti leitourgias tou theatrou 'Kefalos' kai tin ensomatosi ton Eptanison sto 'Vasileion tis Ellados,'" *Polyphonia* 23 (Fall 2013), 90–132, and *Polyphonia* 24 (Spring 2014), 77–107.

15. One of these instances occurred in 1867, when the Corfu Philharmonic Society assumed responsibility for Corfu's theater for 1867–1868 and commissioned the operas *The Parliamentary Candidate*, by Spiridon Xindas (the first full-scale opera in Greek), and *Fior di Maria*, by Pavlos Carrer. See Kostas Kardamis, "They Are My Instruments the Council, the Police, the Lord High Commissioner and the Senate': A 'Parliamentary Candidate' Criticizes the Pre-Unification and Post-Unification Corfu," paper delivered at the Tenth International Panionian Conference (Corfu, 30 April–4 May 2014), to be published.

16. The Corfu Reading Society's libretto collection, the Italian musical journals, and the police archives (General State Archives of Corfu) are only some of the sources for Italian singers' and musicians' activity in the Ionian Islands and particularly in Corfu.

17. General State Archives of Corfu (GSA-AC), Russoturks 12.
18. *Gazzetta degli Stati Uniti delle Isole Jonie* 531 (18 February–1 March 1828), 4; *Gazzetta degli Stati Uniti delle Isole Jonie* 618 (19/31 October 1829), 4; *Gazzetta Uffiziale degli Stati Uniti delle Isole Jonie* 57 (19/31 January 1846), 14–15.
19. *Gazzetta degli Stati Uniti delle Isole Jonie* 543 (10/22 May 1841), 7–16; GSA-AC, Ionian State 76, 1 (14 January1841).
20. Extended comments are available in Kostas Kardamis, "Nees eidiseis gia ton Ioanni Aristidi kai ti didaskalia tis moussikis stin Ionio Akadimia," *Moussikos Ellinomnemon* 4 (September–December 2009), 4–19.
21. This initiative was active between 1816 and 1823, and its character was that of a concert club with limited educational activity. More information can be found in Stelios Tzerbinos, *Filarmonika Zakynthou* (Zante, 1996).
22. With regard to these institutions, see Angelo-Dionissis Dembonos, *I Filarmoniki Scholi Kefalonias (1838–1940)* (Argostoli, 1988); Christos Vounas, *Ta 130 chronia tis moussikis stin Kefalonia (1836–1966)* (Athens, 1966); Antonis Filippas, *I Filarmoniki Lefkados* (Athens: Lefkadian Studies Society, 1985). See also *Gazzetta degli Stati Uniti delle Isole Jonie* 511 (28 September–10 October 1840), 13–14; *Gazzetta degli Stati Uniti delle Isole Jonie* 608 (8–20 August 1842), 11; *Gazzetta degli Stati Uniti delle Isole Jonie* 610 (22 August–3 September1842), 6; *Gazzetta Uffiziale degli Stati Uniti delle Isole Jonie per notizie politiche, scientifiche, letterarie* 3 (11–23 January 1844), 11–12; *Gazzetta Uffiziale degli Stati Uniti delle Isole Jonie* 12 (10– 22 March 1845), 8.
23. The tables of the lodge's members are published in Panagiotes Kritikos, *Peri tous tektonas, ton tektonismon kai tin eisforan ton eis tous agonas tou Ethnous* (Athens, 1971), 239, 241, 244, 246.
24. For an overview see Kostas Kardamis, "British Regimental Bands: A Corfu Connection (1814–1864)," *The Brass Herald* 31 (December 2009–January 2010), 54–55.
25. Indicatively, T. S. Hughes, *Travels in Greece and Albania*, 2 vols. (London: Colburn and Bentley, 1830), ii, 63.
26. *Alitheia*, 27 May 1906, 2.
27. More biographical information for most of the following composers can be found in the respective entries of the online version of *The New Grove Dictionary of Music and Musicians* and those of *Die Musik in Geschichte und Gegenwart* (Kassel und Basel: Bärenreiter, 1999).
28. For an overview of Mantzaros's life and works, see Kostas Kardamis, *Nikolaos Halikiopoulos Mantzaros* (Athens: Fagotto Books, 2015).
29. Claudio Sartori, *I libretti italiani a stampa dalle origini al 1800*, 7 vols. (Cuneo: Bertola & Locatelli, 1990), i, 118–119, n.1116 and Indici I, 33. See also the original libretto: *Gli amanti confusi o sia Il bruto fortunato, farsetta per musica da rappresentarsi nel Teatro di San Giacomo in Corfù il Carnovale 1791* (Venezia, 1791), 4.
30. Karl Proske, "Neue musikalische Untersuchungsreise in Italien," *Allgemeine Musikalische Zeitung* 21 (25 May 1836), 333–337: 333.
31. J.A. de La-Fage, *Memoria intorno la vita e le opere di Stanislao Mattei* (Bologna: Jacopo Marsigli, 1840), 46.
32. For a brief discussion see Kostas Kardamis, "The Music of the Ionian Islands and Its Contribution to the Emergence of 'Greek National Music,'" in *The Ionian Islands: Aspects of Their History and Culture*, edited by Anthony Hirst

and Patrick Sammon (Newcastle upon Tyne: Cambridge Scholars Publishing, 2014), 340–366: 352–366.

33. See Kostas Kardamis, "Un Italiano in Corcira: Severiano Fogacci's Music-Related Activities during His Exile in Corfù (1831–1846)," in the online version of the journal *Moussikos Loghos* (Fall 2012), http://m-logos.gr/issues/i0000/. Fogacci was also the librettist of the comic opera *Il ciarlatano preso per principe*, which was set to music again by Padovas in 1840.

34. For a detailed overview of Karrer's life and works, see Avra Xapapadakou, *Pavlos Karrer* (Athens: Fagotto Books, 2013).

35. Leotsakos, *Spiros Samáras*; Kostas Kardamis (ed.), *Spyridon-Filiskos Samáras: Epeteiakos tomos gia ta 150 chronia apo ti gennisi tou* (Corfu: Corfu Philharmonic Society, 2011). See also Alan Mallach, *The Autumn of Italian Opera: From Verismo to Modernism* (Boston: Northeastern University Press, 2007), 95, 212, 214, 226, 391, and Andrea Sessa, *Il melodramma italiano (1861–1900)* (Firenze: Olschki, 2003), 424–425.

36. More information on Rodotheatos is available in Kostas Kardamis, "Greece and Symphonism: The Case of Dionysios Rodotheatos through His Symphonic Poem *Atalia* (for Wind Band), 1879," in *Six Essays for the Corfu Philharmonic Society* (Corfu: Corfu Philharmonic Society, 2010), 111–126; and "Dionyssios Rodotheatos, *Oitona* (1876): A Gaelic Legend in Corfu," presentation at the interdepartmental colloquium *Ancient Myths and Music* (Aristotle University of Thessaloniki, 21–22 October 2012). Published in the conference's Proceedings, available online at the website of the Hellenic Musicological Society (http://musicology.mus.auth.gr/publications), 83–96.

37. An overview can be found in Haris Xanthoudakis, "Composers, Trends and the Question of Nationality in Nineteenth-Century Musical Greece," *Nineteenth-Century Music Review* 8/1 (June 2011), 41–55. See also Kardamis, "The Music of the Ionian Islands."

38. See Kostas Kardamis, "Ptyhes tou gynaikeiou pianismou sta Eptanisa tou 19ou aiona," *Moussikologia* 21, 333–348, and extended version in *Ionika Analekta* 3 (2013), 65–81.

39. See Giorgos Kousouris, *Elena Angri: Enas agnostos thrylos tou lyrikou theatrou* (Munich, 1999), and Kostas Kardamis, "Angri [D'Angri], Elena [Nazarena, Mattia, Catterina]," in the online version of the *New Grove Dictionary of Music and Musicians* (www.grovemusic.com).

40. Information in Giorgos Leotsakos, *Pavlos Karrer: Apomnimoneuta kai Ergographia* (Athens: Benaki Museum–Ionian University, Department of Music, 2003). See also Lountzis, *I Zakynthos meta moussikis*, 401–406.

41. Indicative titles in Kardamis, "The Music of the Ionian Islands," 350.

42. A description of the Ionian Islands practice is found in Baron Emmanouel Theotokis, *Details sur Corfou* (Corfu, 1826), 82.

43. The respective entry of the *Grande Dizionario Italiano-Franchese* (Milano, 1841) is extremely interesting; "Orecchio": ". . . Cantare a orecchio, dicesi Del cantar senza cognizione dell'arte, ma solamente accordando la voce coll' armonia udita dall'orecchio, che anche si dice Cantare a aria. *Chanter d'oreille*."

44. Photographic evidence in private archives suggests that, at least during the late nineteenth century, there were cases in which the ensembles consisted of violin and lute, possibly played by musicians specially engaged from the mainland.

45. Ludwig Salvador, Archduke of Austria, *Zante: Allgemeiner Theil* (Prag: Heinrich Mercy Sohn, 1904), 391–392.

40 *Kostas Kardamis*

46. Ermannos Lountzis, *Peri tes politikes katastaseos tes Eptanesou epi Eneton* (Athens, 1856), 176, 186.
47. "Kerkyra" is the name of Corfu in Greek. The music of the opera *Kerkyra* was by Joseph Schlar, and its libretto was by Joseph Lauf (the premiere took place in Berlin, at the Royal Opera House, on 27 June 1912).
48. *Les Communiqués des Alliés*, the newspaper of the Entente forces published in Corfu during World War I, offers important information about the era's opera activity, which remains to be fully explored. Nonetheless, it should be remarked that operas such as *Aida, Carmen, La Gioconda, Madama Butterfly, Othello, La Bohême, Lorelay, Fedora, Rigoletto, La Tosca, Lucia di Lamermoor, La Traviata, Un Ballo in Maschera, L'Amico Fritz, Ruy Blas*, and *Mefistofele* were performed in Corfu between 1917 and 1919.
49. *Les Communiqués des Alliés* 90 (18 February 1917), 2, and 90 (18 February 1917), 2.
50. *Les Communiqués des Alliés* 178 (17 May 1917), 2, and 372 (28 November 1917), 2.
51. Indicatively, *Les Communiqués des Alliés* 132 (1 April 1917), 2; 178 (17 May 1917), 2; and 707 (31 October 1918), 3.
52. *Les Communiqués des Alliés* 376 (2 December 1917), 2, and 643 (27 August 1918), 2.
53. Indicatively, *Les Communiqués des Alliés* 131 (31 March 1917), 2, and 145 (14 April 1917), 2.
54. *Les Communiqués des Alliés* 258 (6 May 1917), 2.
55. The importance of music for the Serbs refugees is further underlined by the reorganization of the Orchestra of the Royal Guards in Corfu, where they managed to find new instruments and performed in its theater prior to moving to Thessaloniki. See Katarina Tomasevich, "Musical Life in Serbia in the First Half of the 20th Century: Institutions and Repertoire," in *Serbian and Greek Art Music: A Patch to Western Music History*, edited by Katy Romanou (Bristol: Intellect, 2009), 33–53: 37. Some additional evidence regarding the music activity of Serbians in Corfu can be found in the city's Serbian Museum.
56. *Les Communiqués des Alliés* 348 (4 November 1917), 3. The opera premiered in 1876 and, despite the internationalism of its texture, became a symbol of Illyrian nationalism. See Jim Samson, *Music in the Balkans* (Leiden: Brill, 2013), 243–245.
57. *Les Communiqués des Alliés* 376 (2 December 1917), 2.
58. *Les Communiqués des Alliés* 641 (25 August 1918), 2, and 659 (12 September 1918), 2 (the latter concerning works by the emblematic Serbian composer Josip Marinkovich).
59. For a profound and multileveled insight, see Samson, *Music in the Balkans*. A particular focus on the music in Serbia is found in Romanou (ed.), *Serbian and Greek Art Music*, 13–96.
60. *Les Communiqués des Alliés* 348 (4 November 1917), 3.
61. *Les Communiqués des Alliés* 634 (18 August 1918), 2.
62. *Les Communiqués des Alliés* 643 (27 August 1918), 2.
63. Indicatively, *Les Communiqués des Alliés* 644 (28 August 1918), 2; 651 (4 September 1918), 2; and 659 (12 September 1918), 2.
64. *Les Communiqués des Alliés* 641 (25 August 1918), 2.
65. For an overview regarding the World War II era, see Natasa Panayi, *Moussiki kai propaganda stin Kerkyra kata tin fasistiki katochi (1941–1943)*, bachelor's dissertation (Corfu: Ionian University Music Department, 2015).

4 The Sailors' Chord

Comparative Research on Traditional Singing in the Quattro Province, the Ionian Islands, and Dalmatia

Jakša Primorac

Introduction

This chapter presents the findings of comparative research on specific traditional homophonic singing and complementary popular vocal-instrumental music as practiced in three regions: (1) *Cori d'osteria* from the Quattro Province area of the northwestern Apennines and some older types of popular music of northern Italy; (2) traditional *kantades*, *arietes*, and *arekia* from the Greek Ionian Islands; and (3) Dalmatian *klapa* from Croatia. In musical (sound) structure and aesthetics, these types of musical expressions are quite similar, almost identical in many respects. Also, they are mutually akin in various social and cultural elements, even though their verses are set in different languages and there are no significant sociocultural connections among the three areas nowadays. However, the fact that parts of Italy, Greece, and Croatia were much more connected in the distant past than they are today makes one assume that these types of music could have shared the same origins.

After passing through different processes of transformation and conservation during the twentieth and the beginning of the twenty-first centuries, these musical expressions presently occupy diverse positions in terms of status, influence, and popularity on local, regional, national, and international stages and in the media. Nowadays, they act as the main musical brands of their own regions. That is why it is exceptionally interesting to compare various aspects of their contemporary performances, as well as the musical worlds of their social formations.

Six Shared Elements of Traditional Singing in the Quattro Province, the Ionian Islands, and Dalmatia

My previous archival and Internet research revealed a multitude of specific musical and sociocultural ties in the northeastern Adriatic area between Dalmatian and Italian folk over the past four centuries (Primorac 2012). Many written sources and audiovisual material from YouTube confirmed that specific chordal singing, dating from the late eighteenth and early nineteenth centuries, is traceable from northern Italy to Dalmatia. Melodic and harmonic structure, as well as some elements of performance style, remained basically the same in Italy and Dalmatia until recently. But, YouTube as a fascinating source of music did not let me conclude the research at that point. During the past four years, I came upon many audiovisual examples from the Ionian Islands in western Greece. Ionian songs are musically quite similar to the Dalmatian *klapa* songs, even more so than the songs from northern Italy. This finding additionally supports my "Adriatic" theory about the roots of *klapa* singing because the Ionian Islands, like Dalmatia, were closely connected to the northern Adriatic coast of Italy in the eighteenth and nineteenth centuries. Here, I wish to mention that at that time Dalmatia and the Ionian Islands were also linked economically and culturally to some extent.

While searching the Internet, I compared sound structures and performance practices in three different areas. I noticed very remarkable similarities that can be traced to a specific music style that appeared in northern Italy, probably in the eighteenth or at the latest in the early nineteenth century (see section "Historical Dilemmas"). In every aspect I compared, there is a certain level of similarity, to a lesser or greater degree, depending on various elements of the sound structure, text, and performance style. Here, I identify six characteristics of traditional singing commonly observed in the Quattro Province, the Ionian Islands, and Dalmatia:[1]

1. *Melodic structure* (particularly, the descending endings from seventh to third degree in the major mode)
2. *Harmonic structure* (chordal homophony, singing in thirds in the upper voices; bass accentuating the basic harmonic functions; baritone filling the chord in four-part style)
3. *Lyric love songs* (originating mostly in the Middle Ages, Renaissance, and Baroque)
4. *Performance context* (basically historical *serenate* and *mattinate* performed to court and entertain young women)
5. *Performance style* (open emotionality, legato phrasing, accentuation on the vowels, emphasis on chordal fusion, distinctive ornamenting of melody)
6. *Unidirectional musical influence* (from Italy to Greece and Croatia, as no information is available about the reverse course).

Regarding the melodic structure, almost all songs are in the major mode. Many Croatian and Greek nineteenth- and twentieth-century researchers emphasize that the influence of the Italian melodic concept in Dalmatian and Ionian towns resides in the endings of the melodic lines of the leading voice, which often descends from the seventh to the third degree, that is, into the third above the tonic of the major mode. Regardless of the fact that stressing this melodic feature might seem to oversimplify the discussion of specific qualities of the whole north Italian, Ionian, and Dalmatian urban melodic style, it seems that it does play a very prominent role, contributing to the impression of sound resemblance among the three.

Another important aspect is the structure of harmony. Male three-part singing was the most common one, but singing in two and four parts was also present. Less skillful men and almost all women most commonly sung in two parts, in thirds. In three-part performances, the melody is sung by the upper voices (tenors) in thirds, while a bass-baritone voice creates triads by accentuating the basic harmonic functions (tonic, dominant, subdominant). A soloist (usually the second tenor) often starts a song, and at a certain point the other singer (first tenor) joins him in upper thirds. The first tenor, who sings the highest part, is the lead. Singers who sing bass-baritone part enter the song later. If the singing is in four-part, the baritone fills the chord, and in all three geographical regions there are similar rules of separating the bass and the baritone parts. In many examples, the whole group starts a song together. Chordal homophony develops mostly in a slow or medium tempo, and the overall sound of the singing groups is very rich and full, often sonorous.

One rather notable but neglected factor is the poetics of the verses performed in all three regions. They primarily utilize typical serenade-like, subtle, and refined love poetry. In Italy, its continuity dates back to the Middle Ages and the time of Francesco Petrarca. In Dalmatia, folk love poetry was intensively created from the second half of the fifteenth century. It was modeled after Italian poetry and to this day has had a remarkable literary continuity. In some parts of Greece, particularly on Crete and the Ionian Islands, love poetry has been also partly modeled on Italian poetry, especially from the seventeenth century on. All vocal and vocal-instrumental expressions researched here, from the eighteenth century until today, basically represent a narrative about love, which is expressed primarily through verses and tunes of songs, as well as by various performance elements. Other narratives include various topics. Many songs are about nostalgia and longing for one's native land. Also, there are economic topics, such as people's hard life and uncertain future in their poor homelands, which force them into seafaring and emigration. It is particularly significant that all these songs, from the second half of the eighteenth century until the first half of the twentieth century, were performed aboard ships and in port taverns where Italians, Greeks, and Croats socialized.

However, the dominant performance context is courting and entertaining young women by singing subtle love poetry to them. In the past, performing *serenate* and *mattinate* in town streets and squares was greatly important. At the same time, similar singing took place in local taverns.

The three music cultures share numerous key elements of performance style. Emotions are openly stressed in phrasing, as in opera. Also, the vowels are accentuated more than the consonants, and generally *legato* is the fundamental style of phrasing. Enjoying the well-performed chord and fusion, in loud as well as in quiet singing, is very important. Singers often add extra vigor to the seventh degree of the melodic line as they do in final chords. The sixth degrees are often preferred as passing chords. Similar ways of melodic ornamenting are also an interesting topic. Finally, borrowing and adopting of melodies was a centuries-old practice traceable from Italy to Dalmatia and Greece, not the other way around.[2]

The enduring and continuous popularity of very similar musical expressions in the three regions demonstrates similarity of musical taste, as well as similar logic in the composition of new songs and harmonization of the old ones. Should one conduct an experiment consisting of translating songs from different countries into a local language, I am convinced that the majority of such songs would be accepted and perceived as local in all three regions. Nobody would feel that, stylistically, these songs had different origins. Also, should one look back to the 1950s or, even better, to the 1930s, visiting the three regions under discussion, I believe that one would find that spontaneous traditional singing in all three was very similar, almost identical.

The musical domination of northern Italy over the Ionian Islands and Dalmatia is also apparent in folk music terminology used in the Croatian and Greek dialects, which derives from the Italian. A singer is sometimes called *kantadur* in Dalmatia or *kantadoros* (κανταδόρος) in the Ionian Islands, similar to the Venetian word *cantador*. On the Ionian Islands, a love serenade is called *kantada* (καντάδα, from the Venetian term *cantada*) and, especially on the island of Cephalonia, *arieta* (αριέτα or αριέττα, from the Italian word *arietta*). A cappella singing in the Ionian region is called *arekia* (αρέκια), which comes from the Italian term *a orecchio*—by ear (Καταβατη 2015: 18–19). Dalmatians often say *kantanje* (from the Italian verb *cantare*) when referring to singing. The etymology of the Dalmatian noun *klapa* originates in the word *clapa*, the inverted form of the word *capulata*, which in Triestine dialect refers to a group of friends who engage in entertainment and singing together (Buble 1988: 67). These examples should not surprise us if we keep in mind that the Italian language was the lingua franca aboard ships and in ports.

Examples of Melodic Structural Similarity in the Three Regions

In this section, I wish to demonstrate some general similarities of melodic and sound structures in Italy, Greece, and Dalmatia by sharing examples drawn from YouTube, enhanced by simple notational transcriptions.

In order to show resemblances of melodic style in popular and traditional music of the three regions, I have chosen two examples of songs performed with instrumental accompaniment. Simple 3/4 (i.e., 6/8), and 4/4 (i.e., 2/4) time signatures are the predominant figures; therefore, I illustrate them with two notational transcriptions of the leading voice melodies. In both cases, the melodic model is exactly the same. The first example is a refrain motif of triple meter songs. The second is an introductory part of the songs in duple meter. At this stage in the research process, it is impossible to conclude whether one of the presented melodies became a prototype for other melodies by traditional oral transmission or if it was a case of recent plagiarism. Due to great similarities in melodic style and similar logic of composing new songs, it is also possible that these melodies were created independently.

The first example shows (a) the Ionian song *Den thelo na doyleyeis* (*Δεν θελω να δουλευεισ*), performed by Trovadoyroi tis Kerkyras (*Τροβαδουροι της Κερκυρας* 2012); (b) the Italian popular song *Piemontesina bella*, performed by the pop folk group I girasoli (2014), from Parma; and (c) the Dalmatian popular song *Bacit ću mandolinu*, performed by the singer Mladen Grdović (2011 [1996]) and often performed by Dalmatian *klapas*.

The second example shows eight introductory bars: (a) an Athenian popular song titled *Barba Giannis Kanatas* (*Μπάρμπα Γιάννης Κανατάς*), performed by Kerkyraiki Kantada kai Mandolinata (Κερκυραϊκή Καντάδα και Μαντολινάτα 2016); then (b) the song *Dove l'è la Luigina*, performed by the group Coro Montepenice (2014) from the Quattro Province; and (c) the song from northwestern Croatia *Po lojtrici gor i dol*, performed by Marko Novosel and the tambura band Tamburica (2016 [1966]). Regardless of the

Figure 4.1 (a) Ionian traditional song *Den thelo na doyleyeis* (b) northern Italian popular song *Piemontesina bella* (c) Dalmatian popular song *Bacit ću mandolinu*

Figure 4.2 (a) Athenian popular song *Barba Giannis Kanatas* (b) northern Italian traditional song *Dove l'è la Luigina* (c) northwestern Croatian traditional song *Po lojtrici gor i dol*

fact that this motif was not yet recorded in Dalmatian older history, certain northern Italian musical influence is evident in northwestern Croatia as well as in Dalmatia. Today, the song is well known all over Croatia.

Regardless of the numerous musical similarities discussed, I could find only these two examples with almost identical melodic structure in all three regions. In the following sections I focus on various musical connections between these regions that are thus far unknown, including a cappella traditional chordal singing and multipart singing with instrumental accompaniment.

Sonorous Chordal Singing in Dalmatia before 1967 and in the Quattro Province Today

In October 1965, the Croatian ethnomusicologist Jerko Bezić recorded a specific spontaneous male folk chordal singing on the island of Hvar. Two years later, a well-known turning point in that vocal expression occurred: the founding of the Festival of Dalmatian Klapa Groups in the town of Omiš. This event marked the beginning of organized amateur *klapa* singing. The Festival developed entirely new four-part vocal style aesthetics, an innovative style that was soon warmly accepted all over Dalmatia. It changed almost entirely the traditional singing recorded by Jerko Bezić (Primorac 2010: 353–358). The differences between the two styles are remarkable. The Festival promoted a revival of traditional singing. Singers were encouraged to focus on practicing in order to achieve pitch and chordal perfection, which did not exist in extemporaneous singing. The influence of organized *klapa* singing, because of its appealing sound, has grown slowly but steadily since 1967. Step by step, it has become an identity symbol and a brand of Dalmatia and the entire Croatian Adriatic coast. Because of its specific refined sound, rich repertoire, significant public status, and social network, among many other aspects, *klapa* singing is far more influential than similar singing in the Quattro Province and, partly, in the Ionian Islands.

Jerko Bezić's recordings are unique because they are probably the only known recordings of spontaneous chordal singing before the Omiš Festival. Later, Ljubo Stipišić, the main personality of organized Dalmatian *klapa* singing from its beginnings in the 1960s until his death, in 2011, attempted to preserve an old, "pre-Omiš Festival" extemporaneous singing style. From the 1980s until the 2000s, mostly in the surroundings of the city of Split, he would approach spontaneous singing groups composed of older generations and would become their conductor. In order to differentiate them from *klapa* groups, he used the term "pučki pivači," which means "folk singers" in the dialects of central Dalmatia, to describe them. In some aspects of their singing he fostered the "pre-Omiš" style, leaving, for instance, the tenor parts almost unchanged. In other aspects, though, he introduced elements of new "Omiš" aesthetics in the bass-baritone parts. Still, as older singers left the groups and younger ones joined them, the influence of new *klapa* aesthetics slowly prevailed.

In 2008, I accidentally came across traditional chordal singing popularly called *canti d'osteria* (the group is usually called *coro*, or less often *cantori*) practiced in the Quattro Province, a mountainous area nestled in the hinterland between Genova and Piacenza. Since then, I have been following this music formation on YouTube. The striking similarity between contemporary extemporaneous chordal singing emanating from this region and the 1965 Jerko Bezić recordings from Hvar helped me formulate the hypothesis that the contemporary sound of *klapa* singing was created in northern Italy, probably in the second half of the eighteenth century or at the beginning of the nineteenth, and from there it was transferred to Dalmatia, where it was quickly "domesticated" and combined with old love poetry in Croatian and the tradition of performing serenades under young women's windows (Primorac 2010: 285–295; 2012: 259–265).

In the repertoire of the Quattro Province singers, the great influence of Italian popular music is evident, especially the influence of music created before the 1960s in northern Italy, in which triple and duple/quadruple meters were common. However, many songs that in their popular version were characterized by steady rhythm went through major changes in traditional interpretation due to transformations during spontaneous oral transmission. This is especially evident in the *senza misura* meter; in significant changes of original melody, whether in stanzas or in refrains; in *rubato* introductory phrases; in rich melodic ornamenting by tenors; and so on. All these features are very similar—in many aspects almost identical—to Dalmatian and Ionian chordal singings. A good Italian example is the song

Figure 4.3 (a) northern Italian traditional song *Laggiù in fondo a quel boschetto*
(b) Dalmatian traditional song *Gledam bajnu zoru*

Il cielo è una coperta ricamata. In its popular version, performed by Paolo
Bertoli and the Orchestra Italiana Bagutti (2015), the song is in triple meter,
but the traditional singing group Voci di Confine (2013) performs it in *senza
misura* rhythm.

To illustrate sound similarity between the Quattro Province and Dalmatia,
I propose two notational transcriptions in which the melody is alike and
harmony is similar although the Italians sing in three parts, while Croats
sing in four parts. Also, singing in both regions is equally extemporaneous
and sonorous, with similar performance style. The first example from the
Quattro Province goes back to 2009 (traditional song *Laggiù in fondo a
quel boschetto*), performed by Coro Valtrebbia from Bobbio, and the second
example is from Jerko Bezić's Hvar collection from 1965 (traditional song
Gledam bajnu zoru), performed by male singers from the village of Vrisnik
(Bojanić et al. 2011 [1965]).

As an aside, I find it very interesting to follow the sociomusical dynamics
in the Quattro Province on YouTube. The festival in Bobbio, held at the end of
June, and the Borgonovo Festival, held at the end of December, were key events
until 2016. Also, there are many videos of groups singing elsewhere, formally
or informally. Besides, a special feature of this region is the mass gatherings of
spontaneous groups that convene at mountain resorts, such as Monte Crociglia,
in the summertime. This is unthinkable in the Dalmatian *klapa* singing formation because these Italian events imply a completely free music communication
by oral transmission, without previous formal practice.

Until 2015, the dominant group present at various festivals in the Quattro Province was the Coro [Cantori] di Marsaglia from the Val Trebbia region, but after the replacement of the first tenor, it lost its dominance because its new first tenor had weaker musical abilities than the previous two tenors. At the same time, the Coro [Cantori] di Farini became popular. As a consequence of this group's very successful season, in 2016 new festivals were founded in the area of Val Nure, where the group comes from. Its work also inspired the creation of a new mixed ensemble, Gruppo folkloristico I Campagnoli, from Bettola. In addition to these two valleys, the *canti d' osteria* type of singing is also very developed in the region of L'Oltrepò Pavese. For decades, the main performer of this area has been the group Voci di Confine. Today, its members are sixty or seventy years old. Their musical influence remained very significant in their town of Romagnese. A few years ago, the group Coro Montepenice was founded in the same town. This group was supposed to inherit the musical knowledge and skills of the older group.

The contemporary aesthetic of extemporaneous or minimally practiced singing in the Quattro Province is unique. It is strongly based on old tradition, and at the same time it is fresh because many performers are young people. It is a very rare type of chordal singing, one that has not gone through major changes since its origin.[3] One reason for the absence of significant transformations is the isolation of this region, which is not the case with the Ionian Islands and Dalmatia, both famous for tourism. Thus, the following discussion about these two areas will certainly be quite different in terms of music aesthetics.

Gentle Urban *Cantadori* in the Ionian Islands and Dalmatia

Regarding singing in the Ionian Islands, I focus on the three largest islands and their capital cities. Two of the islands and their capitals are eponymous, Corfu and Zakynthos, while Argostoli is the capital of Cephalonia. Different from the practice in the Quattro Province, on the Ionian Islands singing with the guitar and mandolin accompaniment and singing a cappella are inseparable. In fact, vocal-instrumental practice is dominant because the audience finds it more attractive. This trend is also present in Dalmatia. Still, in this section I concentrate only on the Ionian a cappella singing called *arekia*.

Art choral music had more influence on traditional a cappella singing in the Ionian Islands than in the Quattro Province and Dalmatia. Large male or mixed choirs (χορωδία) that, accompanied by full mandolin orchestras (μαντολινάτα), perform regional singing are very popular here. At the same time, the old tradition of extemporaneous traditional chordal singing is clearly evident in smaller male vocal groups. These highly esteemed groups foster a rather different sound from the singing of larger choral ensembles. Also, they often perform songs with the accompaniment of small mandolin-guitar orchestras.

There are not many prominent smaller groups in the Ionian Islands today. Each island has only one distinguished group as its representative, perhaps an important reason why rivalry between the islands is not very developed. In fact, there are no competitive festivals. There were just a few joint concerts, including *Μεσογειακοί Διάλογοι* on Zakinthos on August 27 and 28, 2010, and August 9, 2016, or *Καντάδες και αρέκιες από τα Επτάνησα στο Μέγαρου* on May 4, 2015, in Athens. The leading ensemble and the brand of the entire Ionian region is Tragoudistades tsi Zakynthos (*Τραγουδιστάδες τση Ζάκυθος*). In Cephalonia, within the choir Kefallin-iaki Horodia (*Κεφαλληνιακή Χορωδία*) from Argostoli there is the chamber group *Σχήμα Κεφαλονίτικης Αριέτας* (or *Παραδοσιακό Σχήμα "Λαϊκής Αριέτας"*), which performs occasionally. Cephalonia, as well as the whole Ionian region, is represented in Athens by the group Horodia lyrikon Kallitehnon (*Χορωδια Λυρικων Καλλιτεχνων*). Presently, Corfu lacks a prominent chamber vocal group for secular singing. Some years ago, an excellent group, T'Argastiri (*Τ'Αργαστήρι*), from Corfu, used to perform quite often; however, nowadays, they perform rarely because of the singers' age. Today, the group Corfu voices/Kerkyraiki psaltiki (*Κερκυραϊκή ψαλτική*) is the most famous male chamber vocal group of Corfu; still, this group is primarily dedicated to specific church singing. Older traditions are also fostered by the mixed chamber choir Polyphonikos horos Kynopiaston "Geitonia" (*Πολυφωνικός χορός Κυνοπιαστών "Γειτονία"*), from the village of Kinopiastes.

When Ionians sing *arekia*, their sound is much more refined and precise than that heard in the Quattro Province but generally less refined than contemporary Dalmatian *klapa* sound. Ionian singing is more often loud than quiet, but more experienced groups perform dynamic nuances. As much as the singing from the Quattro Province is similar to spontaneous Dalmatian "pre-Omiš Festival" singing from the island of Hvar, all recordings of *arekia* on YouTube from the 1970s on are very similar to the vocal style of Dalmatian radio groups from the 1940s through the 1960s, which sounded like operetta (Škarica 2006; 2007; Primorac 2010: 326–329), as well as to the performance style of some of the first organized (,,Omiš") *klapa* groups from the end of the 1960s and from the early 1970s (Grgić 2006: 61–67), which imitated to some extent the radio groups mentioned earlier. Since earlier Ionian vocal groups do not sound as spontaneous as Jerko Bezić's groups from Hvar and contemporary singers from the Quattro Province, it can be concluded that they were organized and rehearsed regularly. The

The Sailors' Chord 51

Figure 4.4 (a) Ionian traditional song *Tzatzaminia moy* (b) Dalmatian traditional
song *Ti tvoji zubići*

role of choir leaders in large choirs and chamber vocal groups in the Ionian
Islands must have been crucial in this process.

When comparing the following two sound recordings, one can observe
significant similarities not only in melody and harmony but also in performance style. This is refined urban singing, with arpeggiato guitar accompaniment in the Ionian Islands and guitar and mandolin accompaniment in
Dalmatia. The traditional song *Tzatzaminia moy* (*Τζατζαμινιά μου*), created
in 1971, is performed by the group Kefalliniaki horodia (*Κεφαλληνιακή
Χορωδία* 2014). The traditional song *Ti tvoji zubići*, arranged by Ivo
Tijardović in his operetta *Mala Floramye*, was performed in 1962 by the
male singing group of the Croatian National Theatre and Radio Zagreb
(2014 [1962]).

When compared to the Quattro Province and Dalmatia, the most specific performances among Ionian groups are the ones from the Corfu group
T'Argastiri (*Τ'Αργαστήρι*; i.e., Tetrafonia 2009 [1995]). The first tenor has
a specific falsetto lyric timbre. T'Argastiri sings mostly quietly, gently, and
in a refined manner. The first tenor stands not in the middle of the formation but at the beginning of the semicircle, as is the practice in Dalmatia.
He conducts in the same manner as Dalmatian first tenors typically do. All
other parts follow him, also as in Dalmatia. Their performance style is strik-
ingly similar to the performance style of Dalmatian urban serenading groups
before the first Omiš Festival, in 1967. These Dalmatian spontaneous singers
performed in falsetto, in small groups of five to six singers, under maidens'
windows in piano-pianissimo volume, so-called *šoto voće* (*sotto voce*) style
(Primorac 2010: 390–394). That style is highly appreciated by many modern
klapa groups and experts. Unfortunately, I do not have original recordings
from those spontaneous groups before 1967, but we could consider relevant
the recordings of the first Omiš *klapa* groups from the city of Split (e.g.,
Filip Dević, *Lučica*; see Grgić 2006: 61–67), and probably other towns, since
they certainly based their singing on that local older *piano* tradition.

Multipart Singing with Instrumental Accompaniment in the Three Regions

Although a cappella singing is more important to this research than vocal-instrumental expression, both musical phenomena are connected and inter-laced in specific ways in each region, so it is not possible to understand one expression without studying the other. Therefore, I analyze them here in separate sections, keeping in mind that it is possible, even necessary, to view them as a single musical and social expression.

Even though a cappella chordal singing is very important in all three regions, audiences usually prefer to listen to "lighter" singing with instrumental accompaniment at public events, private parties, and in the media. In many previously mentioned structural aspects, vocal-instrumental music is similar to the a cappella style (see section "Six Shared Elements . . .").

Traditional multipart singing with instrumental accompaniment was recorded in Dalmatia in the late nineteenth and early twentieth centuries. At that time, instruments accompanying the singing were accordion and tambura and, to a lesser degree, mandolin because, according to the nation-alistic discourse of the time, the tambura was a symbol of Croatian national identity, while the mandolin was perceived as an Italian instrument (Buble 1994: 341). Between the two World Wars and especially after World War II, this situation changed because Dalmatia, as a Croatian region, became part of Yugoslavia, where tambura music was present in many other regions. To emphasize and, in a way, infuse with exoticism a specific Dalmatian sound, based on unique melodic style and other characteristics, mandolins and guitars became the common accompaniment for Dalmatian urban sing-ing. There has been little research about professional groups that performed Dalmatian singing between the World Wars; however, just a few years after the end of World War II, Dalmatian singing accompanied by mandolins and guitars became very fashionable. The main promoter of this style was Radio Zagreb, which employed several groups of opera-trained singers who performed such a type of singing. Among them, the most famous was Grupa Dalmatinaca Petra Tralića (Petar Tralić's Group of Dalmatians). The prob-lem with this music resided mainly in the artificial performance aspects of the so-called Radio operetta-like style, which dominated the airwaves from the end of the 1940s to the mid-1960s. Also, the newly composed songs of the time often showed a too "sweet" artificiality in their choice of verses (Škarica 2006; 2007; Primorac 2010: 326–329). However, the *klapa* style of the Omiš Festival overcame these performance and text problems.

Since the foundation of the Omiš Festival, in 1967, numerous mando-lin *klapa* groups were created, but they did not compete officially in Omiš because the Festival favored a cappella singing. Because of their popularity, there is an increased number of mandolin *klapas* today, and there are also some festivals specialized for them, such as those in Makarska and Opatija. Regarding their repertoire, new mandolin *klapas* produce a number of modern songs, often in arrangement with synthesizer and other contemporary instruments. Presently, these songs are far more popular than the songs created from the nineteenth century through the 1960s. These modern *klapa* songs are not much appreciated by "orthodox" a cappella *klapa* singers.

In northern Italy, the situation is quite different. There is a number of Italian pop-folk vocal groups accompanied by orchestras in which the accordion dominates. On YouTube, however, the dominant group is I girasoli (Sunflowers), from Parma. It is not clear if this group still performs, since some of the members are more than 60 years old. Still, the group serves as an excellent case study because of the availability of numerous videos on YouTube, which well represent all popular and traditional music of northern Italy. I girasoli's huge repertoire encompasses a large time span—the entire nineteenth and twentieth centuries—and follows the development of popular music in Italy, especially in northern Italy and various neighboring regions. Even though this popular vocal-instrumental music is similar to Dalmatian and Ionian melodies and verses, the performances of I girasoli are specific regarding harmony structure and performance style. First of all, they often sing in sixths, mixing the traditional homophony of northern Italy with popular chords progressions of different styles and genres of multipart popular music, which streamed from North America to Europe from the end of the nineteenth century to the 1960s or even later. Their harmonic arrangements often evoke those heard in "spaghetti western" movies' soundtracks, thus resulting in a specific hybrid sound. Second, I girasoli are primarily entertainers. All songs, even the sad ones, are performed in an entertaining way. Their videos are simple and somewhat monotonous from a video graphic aesthetics perspective, but in all they attempt, nevertheless, to emphasize a certain entertaining and humorous character of folk music. Quite often they ridicule sad emotions in traditional and popular songs. That is why, in Dalmatia, where this kind of music is much appreciated, and especially in the Ionian Islands, where it is highly esteemed, I girasoli would most likely be considered as "low comedians." Such groups in northern Italy often perform at local feasts and weddings, on radio and television stations, and elsewhere.[4]

In the Ionian Islands, the majority of groups take a very different approach to performance from I girasoli. The most famous group, Tragoudistades tsi Zakynthos, for instance, with mandolin and guitar orchestra, is very dedicated and professional. Ionian instrumental-vocal music is highly appreciated by the audience, and it is perceived as the true expression of the Ionian musical identity. That is why it is not perceived as old-fashioned, as it is perceived in northern Italy and sometimes in Dalmatia.[5] For the group Tragoudistades, this music is their main brand, much more than the *arekia* songs. It represents not only the musical but the whole cultural identity of the island of Zakynthos and the entire Ionian region. Here, the reader should keep in mind that Ionian culture and music are positioned on a very high level in Greek national imagery; consequently, great attention is given to their preservation (Kardamis 2007).

Songs with guitar and mandolin accompaniment are performed by all Ionian musicians either in concerts or as walking *kantades*. This music is performed frequently at male or mixed-choir concerts with accompaniment of mandolin orchestras—an improbable occurrence in Dalmatia, where this type of music is performed by chamber *klapa* groups. However, large male choirs are very popular in northern Italy, so this phenomenon is comparable to the one in the Ionian Islands, which is discussed later. Besides large male choirs and organized chamber groups, there are many informal singing groups on the Ionian Islands that often gather many performers. They walk in the streets performing *kantades* for tourists, with instrumental accompaniment provided by a guitar and either a mandolin or an accordion. Also, there are small groups of two to four or more members that perform in restaurants. Many Ionian interpretations are very similar to those in Dalmatia, but in the Ionian Islands certain influence of *rebetiko*, *laiko*, and other styles and genres of Greek popular music are more or less present in the phrasing of the songs' verses.[6]

Historical Dilemmas

How and when did the common musical chordal system appear in these three areas? Significant musical innovations that occurred in northern Italy during early Romanticism partially developed under the influence of opera, which then became very popular in Ionian and Dalmatian theaters. People belonging to all social strata enjoyed opera performances (Primorac 2012: 261–262; Kardamis 2014: 341–346). However, the birth and development of specific traditional singing cannot be ascribed solely to the influence of opera. At the beginning of the nineteenth century, Dalmatian and Ionian harbors intensified their trade with those on the northern Adriatic coast of Italy. Cultural and musical ties with Venice and Trieste were especially intensive. Probably at that time or earlier, the folk chordal, mainly three-part singing spread into the Ionian Islands and Dalmatia (Kardamis 2007: 357; Primorac 2012: 252–253; Καταβατη 2015: 14–15). It was adopted by Ionian and Dalmatian sailors, tradesmen, and clerks who were staying in northern Italian Adriatic ports. Some Croatian nineteenth- and early twentieth-century ethnomusicologists noted that poor workers in Dalmatian towns imitated

Italian folk melodies changing, often and slightly, their melodic line and adding Croatian verses. At times, they created new melodies in imitation of the Italian model. (Primorac 2012: 253–259) Very probably, a similar process took place on the Ionian Islands.

In the future, it will be important to research thoroughly when and how this musical exchange among Greeks, Croats, and Italians occurred and whether the main intersection of this musical encounter took place on ships and/or in Venetian, Triestine, or other streets, squares, or taverns. My assumption is that it is possible that this three- or four-part chordal type of singing took hold as an urban folk vocal expression on the Italian shores of the northern Adriatic, especially in Venice and Trieste, but this hypothesis should be better examined, as well as the question of whether the chordal singing started in the eighteenth or at the very beginning of the nineteenth centuries.

My research did not solve the question of geographic discontinuity, because the area of the Quattro Province, near the Ligurian Sea, is at quite a distance from Dalmatia and the Ionian Islands, which in the eighteenth and nineteenth centuries were primarily oriented toward Venice and Trieste. Since I do not believe that there was a direct, strong music-historical connection between the Quattro Province and Dalmatia or the Ionian Islands, I presume that the type of singing that is currently practiced in the Quattro Province was spread in the nineteenth and the first half of the twentieth centuries as a popular vocal expression in the large area of northern Italy, especially in the Po Valley, which is between the Ligurian and the Adriatic Seas, and in surrounding hilly and mountainous regions. Also, I suppose that Venice and Trieste were the focal points of this singing, maybe even from the eighteenth to the first half of the twentieth century. It is possible that folk chordal singing in these two cities had a soft and refined sound under the influence of art music, and possibly it was accompanied by mandolins and guitars. All my presumptions derive from the fact that former and contemporary singing in the Ionian Islands and Dalmatia are similar. Yet, in history, there was not any significant and documented cultural and musical exchange between these two regions. The main encounter among them occurred only in or across Venice and Trieste. Further research into historical sound recordings and written sources, especially music notation, in these two Italian cities could possibly provide the final answer to the question about origins of all discussed types of music.

In contemporary northern Italy, traditional extemporaneous chordal singing is best preserved in isolated mountainous areas of the Quattro Province, which is not surprising since such phenomena of isolated areas managing to preserve certain archaic vocal styles are present all over the world (Jordania 2006). Today it is the regional symbol of the Quattro Province, where considerable efforts are in place for its preservation and promotion. Still, one can find on the Internet similar styles of singing dispersed throughout northern Italy. But these are mostly examples of isolated instances. The greatest number of performing groups comes from Piedmont, where three subregions are representative of traditional chordal singing: (1) the entire Cuneo province (groups: Cantori di Venasca, Socio d'la bira, Gruppo "Dal vej al giou"); (2) Langhe (Langa) area, as part of Cuneo province, where the excellent group I castellani performs, as well as other groups (Gruppo Vocale 4 più 1, Le Raviole al Vin, Confraternita della Nocciola „Tonda gentile"); (3) Canavese area (groups: Coro Morfelli/Murfej, Cantori salesi, Coro bajolese, Gruppo Alpigial). Also, interesting videos have been produced in the Emilia region (groups: Gruppo Emiliano from Bologna, Coro Scariolanti from Marzabotto, Gruppo emiliano di canto spontaneo from Reggio Emilia), and Trento (groups: I cantori di Vermei and Vecchie tradizioni cembrane). In Venice, there was a group of popular singers in the 1960s (see Bertelli et al. 2016 [1967]) that practiced chordal singing like that of the groups from Emilia. Contemporary groups from Venice (Coro Serenissima, I Gatti de Venessia), and other parts of the Veneto region (El Canfin, Cantori da filò, Coro Oio) sing mostly in two parts in thirds, whether they perform a cappella or with instrumental accompaniment.

Also, we could discuss when and how this specific vocal expression ceased to be popular in some regions of northern Italy. It probably happened between the two World Wars, when extemporaneous chordal singing was replaced by organized male and, to some extent, female and mixed choirs, especially by the so-called *cori alpini* and, after World War II, by popular groups such as I girasoli. Large male choirs are a dominant tradition of northern Italy. They are so popular that they exist even in the smallest and most remote of villages. This specific choral culture is very different musically from the Croatian male choirs because the Italians perform a plethora of arrangements of traditional and popular songs, whereas in Croatia, choirs usually perform more complex compositions that are not part of folk traditions.[7] The songs performed by choirs in northern Italy are commonly performed in Croatia by *klapa* groups in the south or tambura bands in the north. Arrangements of traditional and popular songs for Italian male choirs, with their complex harmonic structure in lower parts, are set apart from the simple traditional homophony present in the Quattro Province. Besides, choir singers train their voices differently, since the falsetto timbre of the tenors and overall "soft" sound of the choir are preferred. This vocal aesthetic is very different from the sonorous guttural style of singing in the Quattro Province. Today, on informal occasions northern Italian choirs sing rehearsed four-part arrangements or popular songs in two parts in thirds, usually accompanied by an accordion, which is a common folk practice everywhere in northern Italy. In the arrangements of traditional and popular songs for Italian male choirs, tenor parts often keep the traditional melodic concept of singing in parallel thirds, but bass and baritone parts are often complex and polyphonic, so that lower voices cannot spontaneously create third or fourth part in homophony, as is common practice among folk singers in the Quattro Province, the Ionian Islands, and Dalmatia.

The last open question is whether the mandolins were often the instruments that accompanied traditional singing in northern Italy in the nineteenth and twentieth centuries. On YouTube, mandolins almost do not exist in the context of modern northern Italian traditional singing and popular music, where accordions dominate. One of a few examples is the contemporary mixed and male Venetian choir Coro Serenissima, which, accompanied by a small mandolin and guitar orchestra, sings old Venetian songs mostly in two parts, in thirds. Also, the former Venetian group Gruppo Folk San Marco performed songs accompanied by one mandolin, an accordion, and two guitars. Do these two cases represent the continuation of an older tradition? Perhaps. Still, to be sure, thorough research in archival sound recordings, notational transcriptions, and other documents in Venice from the eighteenth to the twentieth century would need to be implemented.

Conclusion

It is my hope that these examples of specific relationship of sound and history have demonstrated a strong historical connection among northern Italian, Ionian, and Dalmatian folk singing cultures from the beginning of the nineteenth century, and perhaps earlier, to the mid-twentieth century. After analyzing examples drawn from the Internet and examining chosen historical sources, I arrived at the conclusion that among sailors of different ethnicities in the northern Mediterranean area and the upper Adriatic in particular there existed a little-known and yet widespread type of vocal expression. At those times, Italians, Greeks and Croats, who navigated together and socialized in port taverns, performed this type of singing. That is why this musical similarity in three different regions can be explained as a consequence of centuries-long mutual maritime connections but also of the long-term Italian political and cultural influence on the Ionian Islands and Dalmatia.

Notes

1. Some of these features in various regions are discussed in the following studies: Jerko Bezić, "Dalmatinska folklorna gradska pjesma kao predmet etnomuzikološkog istraživanja," *Narodna umjetnost* 14 (1977); Mauro Balma, "La polivocalità della montagna pavese," in *Pavia e il suo territorio*, edited by Roberto Leydi, Bruno Pianta, and Angelo Stella (Milano: Silvana Editoriale, 1990); Mauro Balma, Claude Bonnafous, Paolo Ferrari, Luciano Messori,

and Agostino Zanocco (eds.), *Giacomo Jacmon Sala: Suoni e voci delle quattro province (Alessandria, Genova, Pavia, Piacenza)* (Udine: Nota music, 2004); Milana Fabio and Maddalena Scagnelli (eds.), *Le tradizioni musicali delle Quattro Province* (Piacenza: SOPRIP, 2005); Kostas Kardamis, "Music in the Ionian Islands," in *Ιόνιοι Νήσοι: Ιστορία και πολιτισμός/History and Culture of the Ionian Islands*, edited by Μαριάννα Ν Χρήστου and Αναστασία Λερίου (Αθήνα: Περιφέρεια Ιονίων Νήσων, 2007); Kostas Kardamis, "The Music of the Ionian Islands and Its Contribution to the Emergence of 'Greek National Music,'" in *The Ionian Islands: Aspects of Their History and Culture*, edited by Anthony Hirst and Patrick Sammon (Cambridge: Cambridge Scholars Publishing, 2014); Αθανασια Ελενη Καταβατη, *Ιονιο Μουσικο Αρχειο: Ένα ολοκληρωμένο πλαίσιο προβολής και εμπλουτισμού: Πτυχιακή εργασία* (Ληξουρι: Τεχνολογικό Εκπαιδευτικό Ίδρυμα Ιονίων Νήσων—Σχολή Μουσικής Τεχνολογίας—Τμήμα Τεχνολογίας Ήχου & Μουσικών Οργάνων, 2015), 18–19; Jakša Primorac, "*Legatura Adriatica*: Long-lasting Ties Between Urban Folk Music of Dalmatia and Northern Italy," in *7th International symposium "Music in Society" Sarajevo 28–30.10.2010. Collection of Papers*, edited by Jasmina Talam, Fatima Hadžić, and Refik Hodžić (Sarajevo: Muzikološko društvo Federacije Bosne i Hercegovine—Muzička akademija u Sarajevu, 2012).

2. I am aware of five such examples from Dalmatia, but only one from the Ionian Islands—*Le osterie (para ponzi po')/Παραπότζι*. Dalmatian adoptions of Italian songs are: (1) *Nina mia son barcherolo/Milko moja, ja sam mornar—Podno Klisa tvrda grada*; (2) *Me compare Giacometo/Sve su koke poludile*; (3) *La mula del Parenzo/Mlada Dubrovčanka*; (4) *Dove sei stato mio bel Alpino/Ja san majko cura fina*; (5) *Amor dammi quel fazzolettino/Sinoć sam ti kod majke bio*. I'm sure I will discover more Greek as well as Croatian examples in the future.

3. For example, it could be compared to contemporary *a cuncordu* church singing in Sardinia.

4. The scene of pop-folk groups similar to I girasoli from Parma, Emilia-Romagna, is by far the most developed in Piedmont. Here are the names of some prominent groups: Le nostre valli, I tre castelli, I birikin, Orchestra Italiana Bagutti, and the female group Le mondine.

5. On various attitudes toward this music in Dalmatia, see the preceding passage.

6. For example, the song *Εγώ Παπούτσια δεν εχώ*, performed by informal quartet in a taverna at Zakynthos in 2007. (Πέτρος Βυθούλκας and Σπύρος Μανταλάς, Γίωργος Μουζάκης, Βαρθάλης Δημήτρης, 2010 [2007]. *Εγώ Παπούτσια δεν εχώ. Ζακυνθινές Καντάδες*. www.youtube.com/watch?v=kdTVuxD40GI).

7. The most famous north Italian choir is Coro della SAT from Trento, founded in 1926. See their Web page: www.corosat.it. Also instructive are the Web pages of the main choirs' associations: www.feniarco.it; www.cai.it; www.ana.it.

References

Balma, Mauro. "La polivocalità della montagna pavese". In *Pavia e il suo territorio* (eds. Roberto Leydi, Bruno Pianta and Angelo Stella). Milano: Silvana Editoriale, 1990: 247–288.

Balma, Mauro, Claude Bonnafous, Paolo Ferrari, Luciano Messori and Agostino Zanocco, eds. *Giacomo Jacmon Sala: suoni e voci delle quattro province (Alessandria, Genova, Pavia, Piacenza)*. Udine: Nota music, 2004.

Bezić, Jerko. "Dalmatinska folklorna gradska pjesma kao predmet etnomuzikološkog istraživanja". *Narodna umjetnost* 14, 1977: 23–54.

Buble, Nikola. *Glazbena kultura stanovnika trogirske općine*. Trogir: Muzej Grada Trogira, 1988.

————. "Da li je tambura 'hrvatskije' glazbalo od mandoline?". *Bašćinski glasi* 3, 1994: 339–344.

Fabio, Milana and Maddalena Scagnelli, eds. *Le tradizioni musicali delle Quattro Province*. Piacenza: SOPRIP, 2005.

Grgić, Miljenko. *Ljetopisi Festivala dalmatinskih klapa—Omiš 1967–2006*. Omiš: Festival dalmatinskih klapa—Omiš, 2006.

Jordania, Joseph. *Who Asked the First Question? The Origins of Human Choral Singing, Intelligence, Language and Speech*. Tbilisi: Logos, 2006.

Kardamis, Kostas. "Music in the Ionian Islands". In *Ιόνιοι Νήσοι: Ιστορία και πολιτισμός/History and Culture of the Ionian Islands* (eds. Μαριάννα Ν Χρήστου and Αναστασία Λερίου). Αθήνα: Περιφέρεια Ιονίων Νήσων, 2007: 356–365.

————. "The Music of the Ionian Islands and Its Contribution to the Emergence of 'Greek National Music'". In *The Ionian Islands: Aspects of Their History and Culture* (eds. Anthony Hirst and Patrick Sammon). Cambridge: Cambridge Scholars Publishing, 2014: 340–366.

Καταβάτη, Αθανασια Ελενη. *Ιονιο Μουσικο Αρχειο: Ένα ολοκληρωμένο πλαίσιο προβολής και εμπλουτισμού: Πτυχιακή εργασία*. Ληξουρι: Τεχνολογικό Εκπαιδευτικό Ίδρυμα Ιονίων Νήσων—Σχολή Μουσικής Τεχνολογίας—Τμήμα Τεχνολογίας Ήχου & Μουσικών Οργάνων, 2015.

Primorac, Jakša. *Klapsko pjevanje u Hrvatskoj. Povijesni, kulturnoantropološki i estetski aspekti*. Unpublished PhD thesis. Zagreb: Filozofski fakultet Sveučilišta u Zagrebu, 2010.

————. "*Legatura Adriatica*: Long-Lasting Ties between Urban Folk Music of Dalmatia and Northern Italy". In *7th International Symposium 'Music in Society' Sarajevo 28–30.10.2010. Collection of Papers* (eds. Jasmina Talam, Fatima Hadžić and Refik Hodžić). Sarajevo: Muzikološko društvo Federacije Bosne i Hercegovine & Muzička akademija u Sarajevu, 2012: 247–267.

Škarica, Siniša, ed. *101 dalmatinska: The Original Sound of Dalmatia, 1950–1960. Izvorni snimci dalmatinskih pjesama na 4 CDa*. CD 11349. Zagreb: Croatia Records, 2006.

Škarica, Siniša, ed. *101 dalmatinska: The Original Sound of Dalmatia, 1960–1970. Izvorni snimci dalmatinskih pjesama na 4 CDa*. CD 11350. Zagreb: Croatia Records, 2007.

Videography

All websites were accessed on January 1, 2017.

Bertelli, Gualtiero, Tiziano Bertelli, Policarpo Lanzi, Luisa Ronchini and Rosanna Trolese. 2016 [1967]. *Canzoniere Popolare Veneto—Nina mia son barcherolo*. www.youtube

Bertoli, Paolo and Orchestra Italiana Bagutti. 2015. *Il cielo è una coperta ricamata*. www.youtube.com/watch?v=xb9WC1EfXC4

60   *Jakša Primorac*

Βυθούλκας, Πέτρος, Σπύρος Μανταλάς, Γίωργος Μουζάκης & Βαρθάλης Δημήτρης. 2010 [2007]. *Εγώ Παπούτσια δεν εχώ. Ζακυνθινές Καντάδες.* www.youtube.com/watch?v=kdTVuxD40GI

Bojanić, Alviž, Ivan Grgičević, Luka Bojanić and other traditional singers. 2011 [1965]. *Gledam bajnu zoru.* Recorded by Jerko Bezić in Vrisnik, island of Hvar, October 23rd 1965. www.youtube.com/watch?v=_c9OVwJginI

Coro Montepenice. 2014. *Dove l'è la Luigina.* www.youtube.com/watch?v=QuTcRTSboqQ

Coro Valtrebbia. 2009. *Laggiù in fondo a quel boschetto.* www.youtube.com/watch?v=NTyjncCzah4

Grdović, Mladen. 2011 [1996]. *Bacit ću mandolinu.* www.youtube.com/watch?v=bV6ejNiCEt0

I girasoli. 2014. *Piemontesina bella.* www.youtube.com/watch?v=5WClr7Muk8E

Κεφαλληνιακή Χορωδία. 2014. *Τζατζαμινιά μου.* www.youtube.com/watch?v=nWCrYMZnqF8

Κερκυραϊκή Καντάδα και Μαντολινάτα. 2016. *Μπάρμπα Γιάννης Κανατάς.* www.youtube.com/watch?v=8FAEyOgE7HY

Male Singing Group of Croatian National Theatre and Radio Zagreb. 2014 [1962]. *Ti tvoji zubići* [arranged by Ivo Tijardović in his operetta *Mala Floramye*]. www.youtube.com/watch?v=erPGc1P8HYo

Novosel, Marko and Ansambl 'Tamburica'. 2016 [1966]. *Po lojtrici gor i dol.* www.youtube.com/watch?v=L-OF6qfHB_g

Tetrafonia. 2009 [1995]. *Corfu is singing—Η Κέρκυρα τραγουδάει [1 από 15].* www.youtube.com/watch?v=2Ps6uJimdYk

Τροβαδούροι της Κερκυρας. 2012. *Δεν θελω να δουλευεισ.* www.youtube.com/watch?v=gcspApycZiE

Voci di Confine. 2013. *Il cielo è una coperta ricamata.* www.youtube.com/watch?v=GWmHSqlaEpM

5 Musicians on the Move in the Early Modern Era

An Instrumental Pilgrimage to L'Aquila

Francesco Zimei

Just as the papal coronation of Celestine V, which occurred on August 29, 1294, in the Basilica of Santa Maria di Collemaggio at L'Aquila, was a key event in the political and spiritual history of the late Middle Ages, the plenary annual indulgence Pope Celestine contextually tied to that place was probably a turning point for the performance of popular music in religious festivals. In fact, in the bull granting this privilege, which directly paved the way for the Great Jubilee of Boniface VIII,[1] the new pontiff—formerly Pietro del Morrone, a long-time hermit dwelling in the mountains of Abruzzi—urged the faithful going to Collemaggio to propitiate forgiveness of their sins by singing *hymni et cantici*.[2]

Apart from its formulaic style, inspired by several sacred and hagiographic texts,[3] this expression, effectively matching the spontaneous and unifying character of the canticles to the sacred context of the hymns, has apparently been the first influential acknowledgment of the use of vernacular songs in penitential ceremonies—an invitation taken literally by local people that gave rise to intense *lauda* singing, significantly enhanced after Celestine's canonization in 1313.[4]

Almost unknown but not less important is the parallel tradition that featured these celebrations. Dozens of instrumentalists coming from many parts of Italy and from even abroad played along city roads on the octave preceding the feast.

The earliest attestation of what sources regularly refer to as *soni* dates back to May 19, 1351, when the community of L'Aquila co-opted Celestine among its patron saints. On that very occasion, according to the coeval chronicler Buccio di Ranallo, the minstrels expected to play arrived in a smaller number than usual because of some contingencies,[5] a fact that implies the existence of an already established custom clearly referable to the indulgence itself.

After the establishment of the patronal feast, the *soni* took place regularly with identical procedures both in May and in August. All musicians,

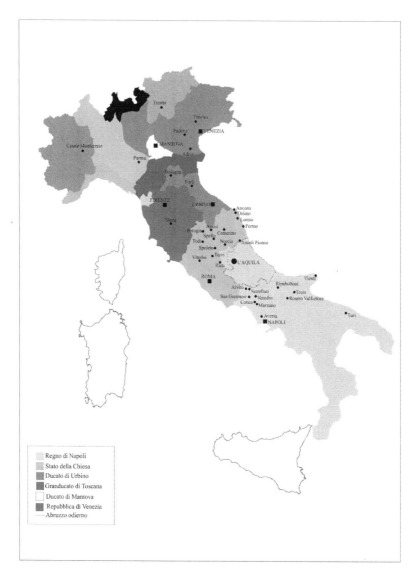

Figure 5.1 An overview of the origins of the Italian *sonatori*

gathering first at Piazza Santa Margherita, had to walk and play twice a day along an established route of about 3.5 kilometers, intended to connect the town quarters to the Basilica of Santa Maria di Collemaggio, located *extra moenia*.

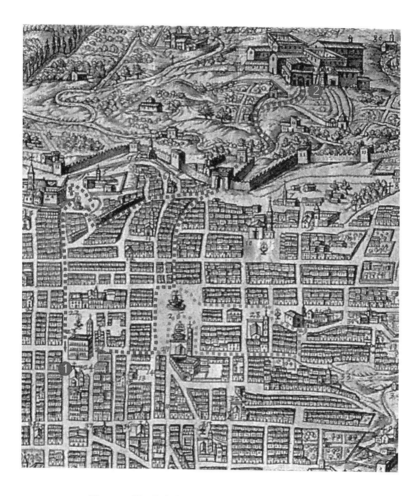

■■■■■■■	Itinerary on May festivals
■■■■■■■	Additional path on August festivals
①	Town hall
②	Basilica of Santa Maria di Collemaggio

Figure 5.2 The path of the *soni* reported on a city map of L'Aquila by Scipione
Antonelli engraved by Giacomo Lauro (Rome, 1622)

The presence of instrumental music in the devotional ceremonies of
Renaissance Europe is widely known. Just consider the role of civic ensembles and minstrels' guilds, with their ample range of combinations, in the
Corpus Christi or in other general processions,[6] as well as the *Salve* (or *Lof*

in Dutch) services in honor of the Virgin Mary performed in the Low Countries after Vespers in the days of free market.[7]

What is certainly surprising about the Aquilan *soni*, making them probably unique among such kind of events, is the dimension and persistence of a tradition deeply felt by worshipers and thus institutionally charged to the municipality, enough to have left a precise trace in the city's payrolls. The extant ledgers, preserved in the local Archivio di Stato and dating from the third quarter of the fifteenth century, cover, with few exceptions, most of the story of the *soni* up to May 13, 1802, when a gradual shift in the political and religious mentality, probably influenced by the French invasion of the Kingdom of Naples, led the rulers to abolish them with the purpose of converting the inherent expenses to public utilities.[8]

In terms of organization and logistics, the musicians reached L'Aquila spontaneously, often according to old family customs renewed at every generational turnover. The meeting point was fixed at the City Hall. All participants declared their name, provenance, and the kind of instrument they played to a municipal officer in return for a credit note. This document would have allowed each participant to collect the fee agreed upon, and a daily meal at the monastery of Collemaggio. At the end of the feast, the

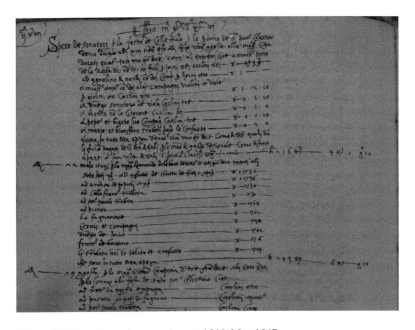

Figure 5.3 Payrolls on the *soni*, August 1546–May 1547

Archivio di Stato dell'Aquila, MS ACA W.37, f. 216v

bulletins were collected, transcribed, and itemized into special sections of the account books, so as to preserve their data.

At a glance, it is possible to recognize the presence of entries regarding both individuals and groups. This leads one to assume that soloists and ensembles were generally arranged each on its own, corresponding, potentially, to different performances and repertoires.[9] But at least in one case the musicians were required to congregate and play all together, that is, in the final procession on the feast's eve that culminated at the Basilica with a resonant performance of the Vespers. Given that most of the musicians were illiterate, thus unable to play *colla parte*, it is likely that their involvement in the liturgy consisted of performance of interludes or improvisations on Gregorian versets—according to the practice of the *alternatim*—rather than doubling the singers.[10]

Regarding payrolls, it is useful to report briefly about the status of these *sonatori*, because their results varied according to different descriptions. Among them we find professional instrumentalists, such as civic or palace trumpeters and drummers (for examples, heralds from Siena, Ascoli, Osimo, Montereale, Terni, or L'Aquila itself; or in the service of Restaino Cantelmo, Count of Popoli, Fabrizio Colonna, Count of Tagliacozzo, and Franciotto Orsini, Lord of Monterodondo), as well as *piffari* active in relevant urban or court areas (e.g., Roma, Spoleto, Urbino, Rieti, Sulmona, Chieti, four "vassalli del signor Marchese"). In addition, there was a large number of part-time ensembles, mainly bands and consorts involving

Figure 5.4 An amateur musician of the western Abruzzi and his real work tool

From the land register of Canistro (1746). Archivio di Stato dell'Aquila, MS Catasti 174, f. 72r

relatives or colleagues—the latter, marked by the presence of *mastri*, flourished especially in the craftsmen environment—accustomed to supplement their income as occasional players.

As for individuals, besides minstrels, *cantimpanca*, such as Giovanni Giacomo Sacco, alias "il Cieco di Mozzaniga," who was active in the Venetian marketplace as a bookseller and charlatan, or Fra' Stoppino from Lanciano, respectively recorded in August 1566 and May 1574—and habitual buskers like the Aquilan Bonsonacchia with his tambourine or the Albanian Prente playing a *ceterone*—it is not uncommon to also detect names of amateurs, even of rural origin, as evidence of the cultivation of music in all social circles.

Considering the documentation of the *soni* as a whole, such occurrences shed light on more than a thousand popular instrumentalists.[11] This essay presents specific data and statistics relating to the Cinquecento—more precisely, from August 1505 to May 1610—, that is to say, the century in which the accounts reflect more consistently preserved details; 94 full records totaling 463 players. For a comprehensive overview, the Appendix lists the number of musicians and their instruments involved in each feast, distinguishing between groups and individuals.

The search for possible guidelines aimed at tracing these regular migrations may reveal a fairly significant link between the different provenance of the *sonatori* individually or in groups and the instrumental categories they belonged to, a custom, along with the proven oral culture of the phenomenon, that certainly strengthens the concept of tradition.

Focusing on ancient Abruzzi, including Alta Sabina (now part of the Lazio region) and surrounding zones, ancient Abruzzo alone was the area with the greatest density of participants, the use of chordophone instruments was prevalent in the western section of the map shown in Figure 5.5.

A north-south trajectory starting in Umbria shows a higher concentration of plucked instruments (lutes, citterns, guitars) in Amatrice and L'Aquila, while in Sulmona there is an interesting percentage of bowed instruments, which were eventually diffused along the western and southern borders of the region during the Baroque era.[12]

Wind instruments were to be found along two main areas according to the following trajectories: first from west to east, starting at the plateau of Velino-Sirente, crossing Sulmona and, through the Maiella Mountain, reaching Chieti and then the Adriatic coast. Then, moving up to Marche and down to Molise, this itinerary was characterized in the inland zones by reed instruments—*ciaramelle*, namely shawms, and bagpipes or *zampogne*—while recorders prevailed, also in combination with drums, along the coast, especially around Teramo.

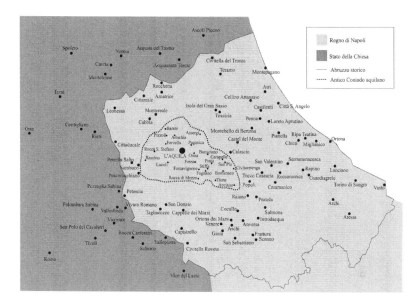

Figure 5.5 Historical Abruzzi and neighboring areas

The second area concerning winds included the southwestern territories along the Via Tiburtina, at least from Rome to the Valle del Salto, with a detour to Rieti: this time, reeds usually joined brass instruments, giving rise to ensembles numbering up to seven players who performed on shawms, sackbuts, and sometimes cornetts.

By translating this information into statistics relating to the individual musicians, Figure 5.6 shows that most of the *sonatori* played chordophone instruments, 41 percent of them consisting of citterns and *ceteroni*,[13] 20 percent of violas, 14 percent of lutes, and 8 percent of guitars, harps, and liras, while the remaining 10 percent are not specified. Next came the brass instruments, including a minority of sackbuts followed by woodwinds with a strong predominance of *zampogne*, ideal for solo performances, in 57 percent of the cases.

On the other hand, Figure 5.7, relating to groups, shows in the payrolls record a tendential equality between homogeneous wind bands and string ensembles, followed by the trumpeters. Nevertheless, there was a small percentage of mixed ensembles of winds and strings or even special combinations such as harp and tambourine, *zampogna* and *lira*, or *buttafuoco* (a string drum) and tambourine.

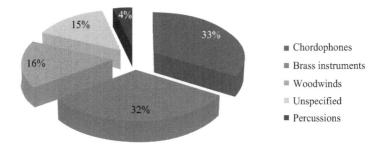

Figure 5.6 Instruments played at the *soni* by individuals (1505–1610)

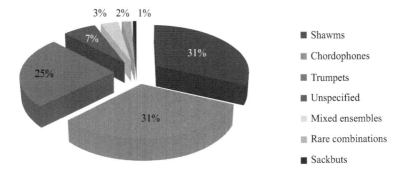

Figure 5.7 Instruments played at the *soni* by groups (1505–1610)

Considering the broad number of musicians on the move twice a year to and from L'Aquila, the municipality's annual budget for the *soni*, substantial as a whole, amounted to little more than a refund when distributed among the single participants.[14] Indeed, taking again into account the sixteenth century, the average expense *pro capite* fluctuated from ducats 0.73 in the 1510s to 0.29 during the political crisis of the 1550s, balanced to about ducats 0.63 in the 1590s.[15] The musicians' commitment had therefore to rely on motivations going far beyond the prospect of a real gain.

One should return to its original function in the context of the Celestinian celebrations in order to understand the deep reasons for this phenomenon. In this regard, a crucial connection can be read in a municipal statute of L'Aquila issued on May 10, 1434. It regulated, through the appointment of three expert masters for each quarter, a purifying dance in honor of St. Celestine to be performed "per totam Civitatem" for four days before the feast.[16] Of great interest is also the penalty clause imposed against any detractors:

anyone who had preached against this custom would have his tongue cut off and be exiled from the city in perpetuity.[17]

Such a ritual seems to have been preserved as a public event until the end of the Quattrocento and then survived for centuries in a symbolic form through the pure performance of its musical accompaniment. Therefore, the *soni* were substantially dance music. An emblematic example of this feature is found in a couple of pieces significantly titled *Chiarenzana* and *Saltarello de l'Aquila*, published by Marcantonio del Pifaro in his *Intabulatura de*

(A)

Figure 5.8 Chiarenzana L'Aquila from *Intabulatura de lauto di Marcantonio del Pifaro bolognese*

Figure 5.8 (Continued)

lauto (Venice, 1546), a probable legacy of a popular *maniera* typical of the city, spread even outside the borders of Abruzzi.

On the other hand, this brings to mind specific meaning of the word *soni* mentioned by Italian theorists of the Trecento in connection with the *ballata* forms,[18] used at that time on a massive scale also for the *lauda* repertoire. This, definitely, constituted the true link between *laude* and *soni* according to the spirit of the indulgence issued by Celestine V.

Figure 5.9 Saltarello de L'Aquila from *Intabulatura de lauto di Marcantonio del Pifaro bolognese*

Figure 5.9 (Continued)

APPENDIX

Summary results of the *soni* (1505–1610)*

Year	Feast	Total	Detail
1505	P	23	GROUPS: 4 piffari; 2 piffari; 2 pipes & tabors; 4 n/s; INDIVIDUALS: 5 trumpets, shawm, zampogna, tambourine, viola, harp, lute
1506	S	36	GROUPS: 4 trumpets; 3 piffari, including a tambourine; 3 piffari; 3 piffari; 2 piffari; 2 piffari; viola and cittern, 2 n/s; INDIVIDUALS: trumpet, 3 bagpipes, 2 tambourines, 3 violas, 3 citterns, 3 n/s
1507	S	16	GROUPS: 2 trumpets; 3 piffari "et altrj sonj"; 2 piffari; INDIVIDUALS: 6 trumpets, tambourine, cittern, lute
1507	P	18	GROUPS: 3 trumpets; 3 piffari; lute, viola and tambourine; 2 lutes; INDIVIDUALS: 4 trumpets, 2 tambourines, lute
1508	S	32	GROUPS: 4 trumpets and drums; 2 trumpets; 2 trumpets; 2 trumpets; 3 piffari; 3 piffari; 2 piffari; 3 [chordophones]; INDIVIDUALS: trumpet, 2 piffari, bagpipe, string drum, cittern, 4 n/s
1508	P	3	INDIVIDUALS: trumpet, tambourine, lute
1509	P	11	GROUPS: 3 piffari; 4 n/s; INDIVIDUALS: trumpet, tambourine, viola, lute
1510	S	4	GROUPS: 3 piffari; INDIVIDUALS: 1 n/s
1511	S	5	GROUPS: 3 trumpets; cittern and tambourine
1511	P	6	GROUPS: 3 trumpets; 3 piffari
1518	P	34	GROUPS: 3 trumpets; 9 piffari; INDIVIDUALS: 12 trumpets, 2 zampognas, shawm, tambourine, 5 ceteroni, viola da braccio
1519	S	n/s	"*li soni*, id est trumpets, piffari, and many other instruments"
1526	S	39	GROUPS: 3 trumpets; 2 trumpets; 3 piffari; 3 piffari; 2 piffari; 2 piffari; 2 bagpipes; lute and shawm; 3 n/s; INDIVIDUALS: 3 trumpets, sackbut, 5 zampognas, 2 bagpipes, pipe & string drum, pipe & tabor, lute, ceterone, 1 n/s; "a leader of *li soni*"
1539	S	14	GROUPS: 3 trumpets; 4 piffari; 4 piffari; 3 piffari
1539	P	13	GROUPS: 3 trumpets and drums; 4 piffari; 4 piffari; INDIVIDUALS: cittern
1540	S	9	GROUPS: 3 trumpets and drums; 5 piffari
1540	P	4	GROUPS: 3 trumpets; INDIVIDUALS: 1 n/s
1542	S	12	GROUPS: 3 trumpets; 3 piffari; 5 [chordophones]; INDIVIDUALS: lute

(Continued)

(Continued)

Year	Feast	Total	Detail
1542	P	11	GROUPS: 3 trumpets; 3 piffari; 3 piffari; INDIVIDUALS: trumpet, viola
1543	S	14	GROUPS: 3 trumpets; 4 piffari; 4 piffari; INDIVIDUALS: zampogna, tambourine, cittern
1543	P	18	GROUPS: 3 trumpets; 4 piffari; 4 piffari; 4 n/s; INDIVIDUALS: bagpipe, pipe & string drum, cittern
1544	S	26	GROUPS: 2 trumpets; 4 sackbuts; 4 piffari; 4 piffari; 3 piffari; 3 piffari; 3 piffari; shawm and zampogna; INDIVIDUALS: cittern
1544	P	12	GROUPS: 2 trumpets; 4 piffari; pipe & string drum, drum and tambourine; ceterone and bagpipe; INDIVIDUALS: ceterone
1545	S	17	GROUPS: 3 trumpets; 4 piffari; 3 piffari; shawm and zampogna; viola, violone and ceterone; INDIVIDUALS: cittern, 1 n/s
1546	S	18	GROUPS: 2 trumpets; 6 sackbuts; 3 piffari; 3 piffari; harp and 2 [chordophones]; INDIVIDUALS: zampogna
1546	P	15	GROUPS: 2 trumpets; 3 piffari; 3 piffari; shawm and zampogna; viola, violone and ceterone; INDIVIDUALS: viola, ceterone
1547	S	18	GROUPS: 2 trumpets; 2 piffari and zampogna; harp, lira and violone; 4 [chordophones]; INDIVIDUALS: 2 trumpets, viola, cittern, [chordophone], 1 n/s
1547	P	14	GROUPS: 2 trumpets; 4 piffari; shawm and zampogna; pipe & string drum, drum and tambourine; lute and ceterone; INDIVIDUALS: trumpet
1548	S	12	GROUPS: 2 trumpets; 3 piffari; shawm and zampogna; INDIVIDUALS: trumpet, viola, harp, lute, 1 n/s
1548	P	19	GROUPS: 2 trumpets; 4 piffari; 3 piffari; shawm, zampogna, viola and violone; INDIVIDUALS: trumpet, shawm, zampogna, cittern, 2 n/s
1549	S	33	GROUPS: 2 trumpets; 6 sackbuts; 4 piffari; shawm, 2 zampognas and guitar; shawm, viola and [chordophone]; harp and [chordophone]; 3 n/s; 2 n/s; INDIVIDUALS: 2 trumpets, zampogna, violetta, cittern, 2 n/s
1549	P	23	GROUPS: 2 trumpets; 5 piffari; 4 piffari; shawm and cittern; 4 n/s; INDIVIDUALS: 2 piffari, zampogna, tambourine, cittern, 1 n/s
1550	S	24	GROUPS: 2 trumpets; 3 piffari; 3 piffari; 3 piffari; 3 piffari; 2 piffari; 2 [chordophones]; INDIVIDUALS: trumpet, shawm, zampogna, harp, cittern, lute

Year	Feast	Total	Detail
1550	P	33	GROUPS: 2 trumpets; 4 piffari; 4 piffari; zampogna, harp and lute; lute and 2 [chordophones]; viola and violone; INDIVIDUALS: trumpet, tambourine, 2 piffari, zampogna, 2 arpe, cittern, guitar, violone, [chordophone], 4 n/s
1551	S	24	GROUPS: 2 trumpets; 2 trumpets; 5 piffari; 3 piffari; harp, lute and 2 [chordophones]; 2 n/s; INDIVIDUALS: bagpipe, zampogna, tambourine, cittern, ceterone, [chordophone]
1551	P	43	GROUPS: 2 trumpets; 5 piffari; 4 piffari; 4 piffari; 3 piffari; zampogna and lira; harp and 3 [chordophones]; violone and 3 [chordophones]; 4 [chordophones]; 4 n/s; 2 n/s; 2 n/s; INDIVIDUALS: trumpet, tambourine, 1 n/s
1552	S	31	GROUPS: 2 trumpets; 6 piffari; 4 piffari; 3 piffari; 3 piffari; shawm and 3 n/s; shawm, [chordophone], and 1 n/s; shawm and zampogna; harp and [chordophone]; INDIVIDUALS: trumpet, cittern
1553	S	30	GROUPS: 2 trumpets; 4 piffari; 4 piffari; 3 piffari; 2 piffari; 2 piffari; 2 piffari; 4 n/s; INDIVIDUALS: 2 piffari, 2 zampognas, 2 ceteroni, [chordophone]
1553	P	8	GROUPS: 2 piffari; lute and 1 n/s; INDIVIDUALS: shawm, zampogna, cittern, 1 n/s
1554	S	17	GROUPS: 2 trumpets; 5 piffari; shawm, zampogna, harp and lute; 2 [chordophones]; INDIVIDUALS: zampogna, cittern, ceterone, [chordophone]
1555	P	14	GROUPS: 6 trumpets; 2 trumpets; 2 piffari; lute and 1 n/s; INDIVIDUALS: zampogna, cittern
1560	P	6	GROUPS: 4 trumpets; 2 trumpets
1561	P	10	GROUPS: 4 trumpets; INDIVIDUALS: trumpet, bagpipe, viola, lute, [chordophone], 1 n/s
1562	S	15	GROUPS: 2 trumpets; 2 piffari; 2 liras and lute; INDIVIDUALS: 2 trumpets, bagpipe, ribeca, 2 liras, 2 lutes
1562	P	25	GROUPS: 3 trumpets; 2 trumpets; 4 piffari; 3 n/s; 2 n/s; INDIVIDUALS: trumpet, shawm, zampogna, bagpipe, lira, lute, cittern, ceterone, 3 [chordophones]
1565	S	14	GROUPS: 2 trumpets; 2 trumpets; 4 shawms and cornetts; harp and violone; INDIVIDUALS: 4 trumpets
1565	P	13	GROUPS: 3 trumpets; 2 trumpets; zampogna and lira; 3 violas; INDIVIDUALS: trumpet, ceterone, [chordophone]
1566	S	20	GROUPS: 2 trumpets; 2 trumpets; 4 piffari; 4 piffari; harp and lute; INDIVIDUALS: 3 trumpets, viola, cittern, 1 n/s
1566	P	14	GROUPS: 2 cantimpanca [with chordophones?]; shawm and zampogna; 3 violas; ceterone and chordophone; INDIVIDUALS: 2 trumpets, shawm, bagpipe, lira

(Continued)

(Continued)

Year	Feast	Total	Detail
1567	S	26	GROUPS: 2 trumpets; 4 piffari; shawm, zampogna and lira; 3 violas; 2 violas; viola and lute; ceterone and [chordophone]; INDIVIDUALS: 4 trumpets, zampogna, cittern, lute, 1 n/s
1567	P	20	GROUPS: shawm and zampogna; 4 violas; 3 violas; ceterone and [chordophone]; INDIVIDUALS: 6 trumpets, shawm, cittern, lute
1568	S	25	GROUPS: 2 trumpets; 5 piffari; lira, 2 violas, violone and [chordophone]; viola and lute; 2 n/s; INDIVIDUALS: 5 trumpets, shawm, zampogna, cittern, ceterone
1568	P	16	GROUPS: shawm and zampogna; 2 violas, ceterone and [chordophone]; lira, violone and [chordophone]; 2 lutes; 2 n/s; INDIVIDUALS: 2 trumpets, cittern
1569	S	22	GROUPS: 2 trumpets; 2 trumpets; 3 violas; 2 violas; lira, violone and [chordophone]; 2 n/s; INDIVIDUALS: 3 trumpets, cittern, 4 n/s
1569	P	27	GROUPS: 3 trumpets; 4 piffari; 3 piffari; shawm and zampogna; 3 violas; 2 violas; ceterone and 2 [chordophones]; 2 [chordophones]; INDIVIDUALS: 3 trumpets, lira, cittern
1570	S	29	GROUPS: 2 trumpets; 5 piffari; 4 recorders and shawms; 2 piffari; 2 piffari; 5 lutes and violas; 2 n/s; INDIVIDUALS: 7 trumpets
1570	P	23	GROUPS: 2 trumpets; 4 piffari; 2 piffari; 3 violas; 2 violas and lute; lira, violone and [chordophone]; ceterone and [chordophone]; INDIVIDUALS: 2 trumpets, sackbut, cittern
1571	S	42	GROUPS: 2 trumpets; 2 trumpets; 6 piffari; 5 piffari; 4 piffari; 3 piffari; 2 violas and violone; 2 lutes and [chordophone]; harp and violone; 2 [chordophones], 2 n/s; INDIVIDUALS: 6 trumpets, cornett, cittern
1571	P	26	GROUPS: 2 trumpets; 5 piffari; 5 violas; 2 violas, violone and [chordophone]; 4 lutes; ceterone and [chordophone], 2 n/s; INDIVIDUALS: zampogna, 1 n/s
1572	S	25	GROUPS: 2 trumpets; 3 piffari and violone; 3 piffari; 5 recorders; 3 violas; 2 lutes and [chordophone]; viola and lute; INDIVIDUALS: 3 trumpets
1572	P	26	GROUPS: 2 trumpets; 3 violas and violone; 3 violas; lira, violone and [chordophone]; 2 lutes and [chordophone]; ceterone and [chordophone]; INDIVIDUALS: trumpet, 3 piffari, 5 n/s
1573	S	15	GROUPS: 2 trumpets; 2 trumpets; 3 piffari; 3 violas; INDIVIDUALS: trumpet, zampogna, 3 n/s

Year	Feast	Total	Detail
1573	P	23	GROUPS: 2 trumpets; trumpet and 2 piffari; 3 piffari; zampogna and 1 n/s; 2 violas; 2 lutes; ceterone and violone; INDIVIDUALS: trumpet, 2 piffari, [chordophone], 3 n/s
1574	S	29	GROUPS: cantimpanca+1 with chordophone; 2 trumpets; 5 piffari; 3 piffari; 3 violas; 2 violas and violone; viola, lute and chordophone; 3 chordophones; INDIVIDUALS: trumpet, zampogna, 3 n/s
1574	P	29	GROUPS: 3 trumpets; 2 trumpets; 5 piffari; 4 piffari; bagpipe and ceterone; zampogna and 1 n/s; 3 violas; 3 violas; INDIVIDUALS: trumpet, chordophone, 3 n/s
1576	P	4	GROUPS: 2 trumpets; ceterone and chordophone
1582	S	20	GROUPS: 3 trumpets; 2 trumpets; 4 piffari; 3 violas; 3 violas; INDIVIDUALS: 3 trumpets, viola, violone
1582	P	12	GROUPS: 3 trumpets; 2 [chordophones]; INDIVIDUALS: trumpet, 2 piffari, viola, 2 violoni, lute
1583	S	20	GROUPS: 3 trumpets; 2 trumpets; 2 piffari; 3 violas; violin, violone and cittern; INDIVIDUALS: 3 trumpets, viola, 2 violoni, lute
1583	P	22	GROUPS: 5 trumpets; 3 trumpets; 2 trumpets; 3 piffari; 3 violas; 2 violas; ceterone, violone and [chordophone]; INDIVIDUALS: zampogna
1584	S	17	GROUPS: 4 trumpets; 3 violas and violone; 3 violas; 3 violas; INDIVIDUALS: 3 trumpets
1584	P	18	GROUPS: 4 trumpets; 3 violas and violone; 4 violas and lutes; INDIVIDUALS: 2 trumpets, shawm, ceterone, violone and [chordophone]
1585	S	51	GROUPS: 8 trumpets and piffari; 5 trumpets; 2 trumpets; 6 piffari; 5 piffari; 3 violas; 3 violas; 2 violas and violone; 2 violas; 2 violas; 2 [chordophones] and lute; 3 n/s; INDIVIDUALS: trumpet, shawm, lute, 3 n/s
1585	P	27	GROUPS: 4 trumpets; 3 piffari; 2 piffari; 4 violas; 4 violas; lute and violone; INDIVIDUALS: 4 trumpets, ceterone, violone, [chordophone], 1 n/s
1587	S	10	GROUPS: 4 trumpets; 2 trumpets; guitar and cittern; 2 n/s
1587	P	16	GROUPS: 4 trumpets; 2 piffari; 2 piffari; 4 violas; 2 lutes and chordophone; INDIVIDUALS: viola
1588	S	24	GROUPS: 3 trumpets; 5 piffari; 3 violas; 3 violas; 2 violas; INDIVIDUALS: 5 trumpets, viola, guitar, 1 n/s
1588	P	12	GROUPS: 4 trumpets; 2 violas and guitar; INDIVIDUALS: shawm, guitar, 3 n/s

(*Continued*)

(Continued)

Year	Feast	Total	Detail
1589	S	31	GROUPS: 3 trumpets; 2 trumpets; 2 trumpets; 7 piffari; 3 violas; viola, violone, lute and [chordophone]; guitar, cittern and [chordophone]; viola and [chordophone]; INDIVIDUALS: 2 trumpets, viola, guitar, [chordophone]
1589	P	18	GROUPS: 3 trumpets; 2 piffari; 5 violas; 2 lutes and viola; INDIVIDUALS: 3 trumpets, shawm, guitar
1590	S	13	GROUPS: 3 trumpets; 2 violas; viola; 1 n/s; INDIVIDUALS: 3 trumpets, viola, guitar, 1 n/s
1590	P	18	GROUPS: 3 trumpets; 3 violas; 3 violas; 2 lutes; INDIVIDUALS: 2 trumpets, zampogna, cittern, 3 n/s
1593	S	27	"10 piffari, 11 violas and harps, 6 trumpets"
1594	S	n/s	"trumpets and other instruments"
1596	S	26	n/s
1597	S	35	GROUPS: 6 piffari; 4 piffari; 4 piffari; 3 violas; 3 violas; 2 violas; 3 guitars; INDIVIDUALS: trumpet, 2 zampognas, tambourine, 4 guitars, 2 citterns
1600	P	12	GROUPS: 2 trumpets; 2 trumpets; INDIVIDUALS: trumpet, 7 n/s
1603	P	20	GROUPS: 3 trumpets; 2 trumpets; 2 drums; 3 violas; viola, cittern and guitar; viola and guitar; INDIVIDUALS: zampogna, 2 citterns, lute, guitar
1605	S	24	"24 [players] with different fees"
1606	P	n/s	"*sonatori del Perdono* and [civic] trumpets"
1609	S	28	GROUPS: 3 trumpets; 4 violas; 4 violas; 3 violas; 2 violas; 2 lutes; INDIVIDUALS: 2 trumpets, tambourine, viola, harp, 4 citterns, lute
1609	P	16	GROUPS: 3 trumpets; harp, cittern and violone; 2 violas; 2 violas; INDIVIDUALS: 2 trumpets, viola, 2 citterns, lute
1610	S	18	GROUPS: 3 trumpets; 2 trumpets; 2 violas; 2 violas; 2 lutes; INDIVIDUALS: trumpet, tambourine, 3 citterns, viola, guitar

* *Legend*: S = the octave preceding St. Peter Celestine's feast day (19 May); P = the octave preceding the Perdonanza plenary indulgence (29 August); n/s = not specified.

Notes

1. On the historical and theological importance of this spiritual benefice, currently known as *Perdonanza Celestiniana*, there is an extensive bibliography; let it suffice here to mention the studies by Giuseppe Celidonio, *S. Pietro del Morrone: Celestino V*, second edition (Pescara: Editrice Artigianelli, 1954); Arsenio Frugoni, *Celestiniana* (Rome: Istituto Storico Italiano per il Medio Evo, 1954); Peter Herde, *Cölestin V. (1294) (Peter vom Morrone): Der Engelpapst:*

Mit einem Urkundenanhang und Edition zweier Viten (Stuttgart: Anton Hierse-
mann, 1981) (Päpste und Papsttum, 16); Edith Pásztor, "Celestino V e Bonifacio
VIII," in *Indulgenza nel medioevo e Perdonanza di papa Celestino*, Proceed-
ings of the International Symposium (L'Aquila, 5–6 October 1984), edited by
Alessandro Clementi (L'Aquila: Centro Celestiniano, 1987); Amedeo Cervelli,
Fonti di diritto nella Perdonanza aquilana, second edition (L'Aquila-Roma:
Japadre, 1994); Onorato Bucci, "Il Giubileo: Radici bibliche e disegno cristiano,
dall'intuizione di Celestino V al programma di Giovanni Paolo II," *Apollinaris:
Commentarius Instituti utrisque iuris* 70 (1997).

2. See the bull "*Inter sanctorum solemnia*," edited in August Potthast, *Regesta
Romanorum Pontificum* (Berlin: Rudolf de Decker, 1874–1875), no. *23981.
3. It can be found, for example, in the Vespers liturgy, in two Pauline Epistles
(Eph. 5:19 and Col. 3:16), in some Franciscan sources such as St. Bonaven-
ture's *Legenda Maior* (XV, 5) or the *Legenda Perusina* (CIX), as well as in the
sequence *Lauda Sion* by St. Thomas Aquinas.
4. An ample survey of this phenomenon has been published recently in Francesco
Zimei, *I "cantici" del Perdono: Laude e soni nella devozione aquilana a san
Pietro Celestino* (Lucca: Libreria Musicale Aquilana, 2015) ("Civitatis aures":
Musica e contesto urbano, 1).
5. Buccio di Ranallo, *Cronica*, stanzas 855–856, quoted in ibid., 333.
6. On this subject, one can refer to the seminal studies of Keith Polk, first of all,
German Instrumental Music: Players, Patrons and Performance Practice
(Cambridge: Cambridge University Press, 1992). Then for specific researches,
see the monumental book by Osvaldo Gambassi on Bologna, *Il Concerto Palatino della Signoria di Bologna: Cinque secoli di vita musicale a corte (1250–
1797)* (Firenze: Olschki, 1989) (Historiae musicae cultores, 55), or evocative
overviews such as Edmund A. Bowles, "Musical Instruments in Civic Processions during the Middle Ages," *Acta Musicologica* 23 (1961).
7. See in particular Reinhard Strohm, *Music in Late Medieval Bruges* (Oxford:
Clarendon Press, 1985), or Barbara Haggh, *Music, Liturgy, and ceremony in
Brussels, 1350–1500*, PhD dissertation (Urbana-Champaign: University of Illinois, 1988), regarding Brussels.
8. See Francesco Zimei, *I "cantici" del Perdono: Laude e soni nella devozione
aquilana a san Pietro Celestino* (Lucca: Libreria Musicale Aquilana, 2015)
("Civitatis aures": Musica e contesto urbano, 1), 396.
9. One of the rare cases in which the program is perceivable can be read in the
expenses of August 1505, where the musical choice of a wind band from Raiano
is so striking that the officer called them "La Ramancina de Ragiano," with a
clear reference to the famous popular tune *Che fa la Ramancina*, which had
survived in some frottola settings of the period. See ibid., 350–351.
10. Such a solution is proposed, for instance, by Richard Sherr, "Questions Concerning Instrumental Ensemble Music in Sacred Contexts in Early Sixteenth
Century," in *Le concert des voix et des intruments à la Renaissaince: Proceedings of the Symposium (Tours, 1–11 July 1991)*, edited by Jean-Michel Vaccaro
(Paris: CNRS Éditions, 1995), 145, concerning the presence of instrumental
ensemble music in sacred contexts during the early sixteenth century.
11. For the transcriptions of the records, the expenses, and a complete Index of the
musicians, see Zimei, *I "cantici" del Perdono*, 404–505.
12. They are mainly arranged in groups, initially denominated *concerti di viole* but
later on described in increasing detail, with variations ranging from *violina*,

violone, e cetra in 1583 up to what should become the standard seventeenth-century formula: *violino, violone,* e *lira*—namely guitar—particularly in evidence on the Marsican slope and the Conca Peligna (Venere, Cocullo, Aschi, Gioia, Introdacqua, Pratola).

13. The latter is among the first attestations in Italy. On the former chronology of this instrument see Dinko Fabris, "Composizioni per 'cetra' in uno sconosciuto manoscritto per liuto del primo Seicento (Napoli, Cons., MS. 7664)," *Rivista italiana di musicologia* 16 (1981), 199–200.

14. Not to mention the Aquilan heralds, who when they joined the *sonatori* were entitled only to a tip for a drink and sometimes a pair of new shoes for the consumptions of the soles. See Zimei, *I "cantici" del Perdono,* 336–337.

15. See ibid., 400–401.

16. The origin of this collective dance in honor of Celestine—apparently practiced until then in a spontaneous way—could date back to the feast for the translation of the saint's body, brought in late January 1327 from the monastery of Sant'Antonio Abate at Ferentino to Santa Maria di Collemaggio. See ibid., 508, with another reference to Buccio di Ranallo's *Cronica,* at stanza 292.

17. See Alessandro Clementi (ed.), *Statuta Civitatis Aquile* (Rome: Istituto Storico Italiano per il Medio Evo, 1977), 367–368 (Fonti per la storia d'Italia, 102).

18. For instance, according to Antonio da Tempo, *Summa artis rithimici vulgaris dictaminis* (1332), "ballatae cantantur atque coreizantur" (Ballatas . . . are sung and danced as well), "Et appellantur soni omnes ballatae mediae" (In the vernacular, all the *ballatae mediae* are called *soni*). English translation by Elena Abramov-van Rijk, *Parlar cantando: The Practice of Reciting Verses in Italy from 1300 to 1600* (Bern: Peter Lang, 2009), 75 and 76, respectively.

References

Abramov-van Rijk, Elena. *Parlar Cantando: The Practice of Reciting Verses in Italy from 1300–1600.* Bern: Peter Lang, 2009.

Bowles, Edmund A. "Musical Instruments in Civic Processions during the Middle Ages". *Acta Musicologica* 23, 1961: 147–161.

Bucci, Onorato. "Il Giubileo: radici bibliche e disegno cristiano, dall'intuizione di Celestino V al programma di Giovanni Paolo II". *Apollinaris. Commentarius Instituti utrisque iuris* 70, 1997: 511–536.

Celidonio, Giuseppe. *S. Pietro del Morrone: Celestino V,* second edition. Pescara: Editrice Artigianelli, 1954.

Cervelli, Amedeo. *Fonti di diritto nella Perdonanza aquilana,* second edition. L'Aquila-Roma: Japadre, 1994.

Fabris, Dinko. "Composizioni per 'cetra' in uno sconosciuto manoscritto per liuto del primo Seicento (Napoli, Cons., MS. 7664)". *Rivista italiana di musicologia* 16, 1981: 185–206.

Frugoni, Arsenio. *Celestiniana.* Roma: Istituto Storico Italiano per il Medio Evo, 1954.

Gambassi, Osvaldo. *Il Concerto Palatino della Signoria di Bologna: Cinque secoli di vita musicale a corte (1250–1797).* Firenze: Olschki, 1989 (Historiae musicae cultores, 55).

Haggh, Barbara. *Music, Liturgy, and Ceremony in Brussels, 1350–1500*. PhD dissertation. Urbana-Champaign: University of Illinois, 1988.

Herde, Peter. *Cölestin V. (1294) (Peter vom Morrone): Der Engelpapst: Mit einem Urkundenanhang und Edition zweier Viten*. Stuttgart: Anton Hiersemann, 1981 (Päpste und Papsttum, 16).

Pásztor, Edith. "Celestino V e Bonifacio VIII". In *Indulgenza nel medioevo e Perdonanza di papa Celestino*. Proceedings of the International Symposium (L'Aquila, 5–6 October 1984), ed. by Alessandro Clementi. L'Aquila: Centro Celestiniano, 1987: 61–78.

Polk, Keith. *German Instrumental Music of the Late Middle Ages: Players, Patrons and Performance Practice*. Cambridge: Cambridge University Press, 1992.

Potthast, August. *Regesta Romanorum Pontificum*. Berlin: Rudolf de Decker, 1874–1875.

Sherr, Richard. "Questions Concerning Instrumental Ensemble Music in Sacred Contexts in Early Sixteenth Century". In *Le concert des voix et des instruments à la Renaissaince*. Proceedings of the Symposium (Tours, 1–11 July 1991), ed. by Jean-Michel Vaccaro. Paris: CNRS Éditions, 1995: 145–156.

Statuta Civitatis Aquile, ed. by Alessandro Clementi. Rome: Istituto Storico Italiano per il Medio Evo, 1977 (Fonti per la storia d'Italia, 102).

Strohm, Reinhard. *Music in Late Medieval Bruges*. Oxford: Clarendon Press, 1985.

Zimei, Francesco. *I "cantici" del Perdono: Laude e soni nella devozione aquilana a san Pietro Celestino*. Lucca: Libreria Musicale Aquilana, 2015 ("Civitatis aures". Musica e contesto urbano, 1).

6 The Migration of Seventeenth-Century Music Repertoire to the Cathedral of Hvar in Dalmatia

Maja Milošević

Current archival sources are too scarce to throw sufficient light on the quantity and quality of the music repertoire nurtured during the first half of the seventeenth century in the urban centers of Dalmatia, a region of southern Croatia. However, a valuable document preserved in the Archives of the Hvar Cathedral Chapter reveals the musical practice of that period in the town of Hvar, the main town of the eponymous island, which was ruled by the Republic of Venice for some four centuries (1420–1797), as was most of the Dalmatian coast. During that time, Hvar functioned as the main Venetian port in the eastern Adriatic and as a sensitive barometer for all economic, social, and cultural trends in Italy as well as the rest of Europe.[1] The Hvar document, containing an inventory of books and music material dating back to 1646 and 1647, resurfaced in 1992 during the renovation of the Cathedral Chapter Library, and it is now archived under the code signature XXII/4. This source has not been the subject of extensive research until recently,[2] but its contents—various items of literature, drama, poetry, music, philosophy, and theology—could be of interest to a wider circle of scholars in the humanities and social sciences.

For the purpose of this essay, the recorded titles of the music collections formerly owned by the Hvar Cathedral Chapter serve as the starting point for an overview of the musical repertoire in Hvar during the time of the town's cultural and economic rise following a Turkish-Ottoman attack in 1571 and other misfortunes in the late sixteenth century. These currently lost music titles witness the presence and dissemination of contemporary Italian (mostly Venetian) early Baroque musical literature among the Hvar community, thus representing an exceptional contribution to the local history of art music. At the same time, they are of rare value for the study of Croatian music historiography and early Baroque culture in general being the only, thus far, document in Croatia bearing explicit mentions of authors and titles of works available to local musicians and the general public until mid-seventeenth century.

The music titles recorded in the Cathedral Chapter's inventory can be viewed in Table 6.1, which provides data about their hypothetical first printed editions (publisher, year, *RISM* catalog number).[3&4] For clarity's sake, Arabic numbers were added to the titles, which will be mentioned later in reference to certain inventory units from Table 6.1. In order to present more clearly basic data about musical repertoire available in Hvar until the mid-seventeenth century, this essay is supplemented by Tables 6.2–6.5 which offer an overview of the cataloged material listed by composer (Table 6.2), date (Table 6.3), publisher (Table 6.4), and musical genre (Table 6.5).

Physical Description, Dating, and Author of Manuscript XXII/4: Middlemen in Acquisition of Cathedral Chapter Musical Sources

The inventory of books and music of the Hvar Cathedral Chapter consists of a few sheets of paper folded in half and placed inside a thin brown cover to form a little book (30.5 x 11 cm) totaling 44 nonpaginated sheets of paper. In order to make this material more accessible to future researchers, I have penciled in pagination numbers marking as 1 the first written page inside the book cover and continuing with a sequence of numbers until the last page, marked by number 41, including blank sheets. A part of the inventory pages is bound (pages 1–16), followed by unbound folded sheets that form another physical unit inside the book cover (pages 17–41). The entry at the top of page 1 reveals that a cataloging of units was recorded inside the bound part beginning in Hvar on March 22, 1647. However, the larger part of the inventory cataloged in the unbound part—from page 21 on—was recorded in Hvar the year before, on September 13, 1646, thus positing the question whether the dating of the entries in pages 17–20 was displaced in the course of time from the part of the manuscript dating from 1646.

The entry below the date on page 21—*Inventario delle Robbe di me Gio. And*[a]. *Nĕbri D*[r].—shows that the author of the entire manuscript was Giovanni Andrea (Ivan Andrija) Nembri (b. around 1570), doctor of theology, canon and prominent member of the Hvar Cathedral Chapter. After drafting his testament in Hvar on June 22, 1647, shortly after the cataloging of the Chapter's books and music was completed, Giovanni Andrea retired as a layman in his late seventies to the Benedictine monastery of San Giorgio Maggiore in Venice, where he passed away on March 24 1651. Unlike Giovanni Andrea, Damjan Nembri (b. 1584) was absent from his hometown of Hvar practically during his entire life: at age 10, he left to be educated in Venice at the Benedictine monastery of San Giorgio Maggiore, where he completed his studies in 1602, and spent most of his life there as a priest and, later, a prior until his death (1648/49). In 1622 and in the period between

1634 and 1637, Damjan Nembri was a prior in the St. Chrysogonus Monastery in Zadar).[5]

Damjan Nembri holds a prominent place in the history of Croatian music thanks to his involvement as a composer, reflected in his only preserved collection of four-part settings of the vesper psalms, *Brevis et facilis psalmorum* (Venice, 1641). Stylistically, this collection was aligned with the early Baroque types of Venetian church music and built upon "the successive use of late Renaissance and Baroque stylistic devices (the so-called *stile misto*) . . . [which] is akin to the techniques of early Baroque composers active in Croatia like Ivan Lukačić and Tomaso Cecchini)."[6] Johann Gottfried Walther mentioned Damjan Nembri in his *Musikalisches Lexicon* (1732) as the author of a now lost collection of three-part and eight-part masses printed in Venice in 1640.[7] Both collections were part of the Cathedral Chapter's inventory in 1646/1647 as recorded in the section of sacred music, *Spirituali* (Table 6.1, nos. 29 and 31), which could suggest that they reached Hvar relatively soon, within a few years after their publication. Certainly, considering that Damjan Nembri kept in touch with his homeland through his brother Giovanni Andrea, the canon of Hvar, the presumption is well taken that he had a hand in the acquisition of contemporary musical literature from Venice, which enriched the Cathedral Chapter's fund in Hvar. Credit for the completion of the Cathedral Chapter's music collection during the first half of the seventeenth century can also be attributed to the composer Tomaso Cecchini (1580–1644) from Verona, who, after a short sojourn in Split, lived in Hvar from 1614 until his death, in 1644. At first, he worked as the *maestro di cappella* and then as the cathedral organist in periodical service of the Governor of Hvar.[8]

The many years of Cecchini's musical activity in Hvar indicate that he was very well accepted in the community, while his works testify to the solid level of the performance apparatus in Hvar, for which most of his music pieces, consisting of monodic compositions, madrigals, arias and *canzonettas*, psalms, motets, masses, and instrumental sonatas, were composed. A large part of Cecchini's sacred and secular works was recorded in the Cathedral Chapter's inventory, with the addition of two collections that had not been known from the older catalogs and previous lists of his works. His preserved sacred and secular music offers an appreciation of the composer's knowledge of early Baroque compositional and esthetic tendencies, undoubtedly gained by his continuous study of Italian contemporary music that was certainly available in Hvar, judging by the contents of the Cathedral Chapter's music inventory.

If dates and places of the first editions of the listed works (see Tables 6.3 and 6.4) are taken into consideration, music literature was imported to Hvar primarily from Venice mostly during the period of Cecchini's residence in town. The acquired material served the needs of the church and the community at large; however, it is also possible that Cecchini brought part of the collections printed before 1614 with him to Hvar. The titles represented in the Cathedral Chapter's inventory should definitely be consulted for future analyses of Cecchini's work and to determine the importance of his influence on the island's musical life.

Listed Music Titles

Out of the 34 pages the constitute source XXII/4, the titles not referring to the music are recorded on 30 of them, divided according to physical arrangement of units and format size (*f°, 4°, 8°*. . .), which might suggest they were originally issued in printed format. Accordingly, it could be presumed that recorded music materials (at least the majority of them) were also publications, although they are classified differently: secular collections (with exception of a few sacred opuses) are classified according to the number of voices, while sacred works are listed in the section labeled *Spirituali*. Music material is listed in four pages of the catalog[9] divided into eight sections totaling 73 items primarily related to specific collections or, to a smaller extent, to series, while there is only one title referring to an individual composition.

In the inventory, and accordingly in Table 6.1, sections are cataloged in the following order: [page 18] five-part (*A'cinq[ue] Voci*, 4 units); [page 20] sacred (*Spirituali*, 28 units), one-part (*A' Voce sola*, 8); [page 29] two-part (*A'2 Voci*, 1 unit), three-part (*A'3 Voci*, 9 units), four-part (*A'4 Voci*, 4 units); [page 41] multipart (*A'più voci*, 15 units); and an untitled section with items that do not belong to any of the previously mentioned sections (4 units). More information about the contents of each of the mentioned groups will be offered in the pages ahead.

A' cinq[ue] Voci

The section *A' cinq[ue] Voci* lists four collections of five-part madrigals (Table 6.1, nos. 1–4) written by the *Maestro di capella* from Hvar Tomaso Cecchini and by the northern Italian composers Claudio Monteverdi, Teodoro Riccio, and Rodiano Barera. The seal of the sixth book of madrigals of Claudio Monteverdi in the Cathedral Chapter's inventory (no. 2), a collection that contains the composer's last madrigals for a capella singing, testifies that the work of one of the most famous European composers of the early Baroque was available to Hvar's musicians and audience of that time. Monteverdi wrote nine books of madrigals altogether through which he synthesized the highest achievements of the late Renaissance with principles of the early Baroque *seconda prattica*, in which expression was more important than counterpointal rules of the *prima prattica*, and the word was treated as the "master of music"—namely followers of the *seconda prattica* affirmed by Monteverdi persisted in adapting music to meaning and feelings carried by the text, thus creating a music that would light up the listeners' emotions as the main challenge (*affeto dell'anima*). Thereby, music became a language in which any technical compositional devices, whether old or new, was adapted for conveying feelings and ideas emanating from the text.

The blending of late Renaissance and early Baroque stylistic possibilities was, to a large extent, also applied by Tomaso Cecchini, whose first (and only) book of five-part madrigals, which also included arias with *basso continuo* accompaniment (no. 1), was printed in Venice in 1619, during the first years the composer spent in Hvar. Therefore, these madrigals were probably intended for the use of local performers and audiences.[10]

A five-part section contains collections of madrigals by two late Renaissance composers—Teodoro Riccio and Rodiano Barera. Madrigals for five voices (no. 3) of Teodoro Riccio, a composer who worked mostly as a *Maestro di capella* in Germany, were printed during his stay in Brescia in 1567.[11] They represent the earliest publication among all music collections recorded in the Cathedral Chapter's inventory. The lost second book of madrigals for five voices written by Rodiano Barera (no. 4), a composer active in Cremona, can be also classified as one of the earlier publications in the music inventory. Judging by his preserved first book from 1596, Barera most often used in his madrigals for five voices procedures standardized during the sixteenth century, with limited use of innovation as he focused on clarity of text with application of syllabic and homo-rhythmical principle.[12]

Spirituali

Collections of sacred music are listed in 28 units (Table 6.1, nos. 5–32) in the largest section, labeled *Spirituali*, among which the most numerous are motets, followed by psalms and masses, mostly from the first decades of the seventeenth century. Four collections were written by the Venetian composer of secular and sacred music Giovanni Priuli,[13] who is the composer most represented in the Cathedral Chapter's inventory after Cecchini. These works were printed in Venice between 1618 and 1624, during the time when Priuli worked as a *Kapellmeister* at the courts of Ferdinand II in Graz and Vienna. His full collection *Psalmi Davidis Regis* from 1621 (no. 7), consisting of 17 evening psalms dedicated to Philip IV of Spain, has not yet come to light, while it is not clear to which of the two collections of masses from 1624 the item identified as no. 8 refers.[14] Priuli's two books listed under the titles S*acrorum Concentuum* from 1618 and 1619 (nos. 5 and 6) testify that the motets written in the Venetian polychoral style cultivated in the circle of Giovanni Gabrieli, Priuli's mentor, reached the Hvar community, as well as the instrumental forms (written for ensembles up to 12 instruments) sonatas and *canzonas*.

Citizens of Hvar could have also heard compositions in polychoral style through the works of the local composer Tomaso Cecchini, in his eight-part mass *Detta la celeste* and eight-part *Magnificat* from 1624 (both part of his collection *Il terzo libro delle messe ariose . . .* , listed under no. 11), as well as Cecchini's instrumental sonatas from 1628 (in his collection *Cinque messe a 2 voci et 22 motetti, con 8 sonate*; see no. 18), which are considered the earliest preserved examples of instrumental music composed in Dalmatia,[15] although instrumental forms were represented in some of Cecchini's collections, now lost.[16] The two mentioned Cecchini collections, from 1624 and 1628, were recorded in the group labeled *Spirituali* with 10 more of his sacred works (total of 12: nos. 10–20 and 32), masses, psalms, motets, and lamentations for various singing groups, varying from two to five voices, most often accompanied by organ *continuo*. Two Cecchini's titles from this group have their only sign of existence in this Cathedral Chapter's inventory since they were not included in earlier catalogs and lists of Cecchini's works;[17] the first book of three-part singing motets (no. 14) and the third book *Sacri Concentus* (no. 20).[18] The latter, bearing the same title as Gabriello Puliti's collection of sacred monody (*Sacri Concentus*, Venice, 1614), listed in the inventory as well (no. 22), indicates that it was through this work that Cecchini was introduced to his contemporary compatriot Puliti, who lived and worked in Istria.[19]

Among the works from the section marked *Spirituali*, the fourth book of motets for two, three, and seven voices with organ accompaniment (no. 27) should be pointed out, since the author of this collection of pieces focusing on solo melody and cultivation of dialog was Alessandro Grandi, one of the most talented northern Italian composers of the early Baroque, apart from Monteverdi.[20] After the first edition published by Giacomo Vincenti in 1616, another five were published in the period from 1618 to 1637; therefore, it is not known exactly which edition was kept in Cathedral Chapter's music repository in the mid-seventeenth century.

There are no data available in the literature regarding several items from the section *Spirituali*. Two collections of psalms have not resurfaced in their entirety—*Salterium* for two, three, and four voices composed by the almost unknown Eustachio Arivieri[21] (no. 23) and a collection of three- and four-part psalms settings that have no author name and that are mentioned under the title *Psalmi Accademici Affectuosi* (no. 28), which appears to indicate an alignment with the expressive principles of *seconda prattica*. Authorship cannot be confirmed for four-part responsorials for the Holy Week service, either (no. 24), since their titles are not mentioned in the lists of works of either of two composers with the surname Gualtieri (they were probably related), both active in the Venetian area during the first half of the seventeenth century.[22] The titles of two unknown collections can be attributed to two Benedictines who were composers of exclusively sacred music— Serafino Patta and Gregorio Zucchini. Only the first (1609, [2]1611) and the second (1613) books of Serafino Patta's *Sacrorum Canticorum* are known, as they were both published in Venice for the types of Giacomo Vincenti.[23] Yet, the third book, cataloged in the Cathedral Chapter's inventory, is not mentioned (no. 26). Also, the author of the collection of three-part compositions *Canzonette Spirituali* (no. 30) could have been Gregorio Zucchini, who was active in the early seventeenth century in the area around Venice and Padua, although the work is not mentioned among his known pieces of music.[24]

A' Voce sola

The section *A' Voce sola* (Table 6.1, nos. 33–40) consists of eight works for one singing voice with accompaniment by various instruments such as lute, *chitarrone*, *spinetta*, clavichord, Spanish guitar, and organ. They were all published throughout the first four decades of the seventeenth century. Two collections consisting of very early examples of sacred monodies are among them. The first one, *Madrigali e canzonette spirituali* (no. 38) by Severo Bonini,[25] a composer active in Florentine cultural circles and an advocate of new style and monody, was printed in Florence in 1607, and the second one, dating from 1614, was written by the already mentioned Serafino Patta (no. 40).

The remaining six items are collections containing compositions of secular provenance: arias, madrigals, and *canzonettas*. Four volumes of *canzonettas*, simple compositions in couplet-like form using contemporary Italian sentimental verses, are cataloged under one unit (no. 33). They were collected from various authors by Giovanni Stefani, then published in Venice in the period between 1618 and 1626. There is a listing here of Cecchini's first book of one-part madrigals with instrumental accompaniment, *Amorosi concetti* (no. 39), under which title three books were published in Venice between 1612 and 1616.[26] Today these are widely considered the earliest examples of early Baroque monody to have originated on Dalmatian soil and intended for the use of the Dalmatian community. Half of the *A' Voce sola* group consists of books of arias with instrumental accompaniment printed in the period between 1624 and 1636 by Vincenti (no. 34–37). Among them there are three very popular collections from the 1620s written by Guglielmo Miniscalchi[27] (no. 34), Giovanni Berti[28] (no. 36), and

Carlo Milanuzzi[29] (no. 37), composers with similar stylistic orientation and participants in the beginning and development of Venetian early Baroque monody, whose texture they embellished with melodic and harmonic dissonances, chromatics, fiorituras, variations of rhythm, and other means suitable for conveyance of textual content and musical meaning.

A' 2 Voci

Among the Cathedral Chapter's music inventory, there is only one collection for two voices by Tomaso Cecchini, today lost, *Madrigaletti & altri ariosi canti* (Table 6.1, no. 41), printed in Venice in 1623, as the composer's eighteenth piece.[30]

A' 3 Voci

This three-part section contains nine titles of secular music (Table 6.1, nos. 42–50) heralding Luca Marenzio, one of the greatest masters of the Italian late Renaissance madrigal.[31] Marenzio's *villanelas* (no. 43), cataloged in the Cathedral Chapter's inventory, are compositions of simpler couplet-like form, published in five books between 1584 and 1587. These three-part singing pieces, set to popular verses, reached wider audiences thanks to their simpler expression, which allows us to compare them with popular music compositions of today. This entry in the Cathedral Chapter's inventory does not specify which of Marenzio's five books is represented, thus making it less likely that we can determine which edition was once kept in the inventory, since Luca Marenzio's *villanellas* were printed in several editions.

Among smaller number of works composed in the sixteenth century now cataloged in the inventory, there is a collection called *Baletti a tre voci, con la intavolatura del liuto, per cantare, sonare, & ballare* (1594) by Giovanni Gastoldi (no. 49), also one of the late Renaissance masters and a musician working at the House of Gonzaga in Mantova.[32] This collection was widely distributed and republished a few times. Gastoldi's strictly homophonic *baletti* are very melodious and simply structured in two repetitive sections ending with a refrain; they were meant for "singing, playing and dancing," as the title says.

Four collections of *canzonettas* by the Siena nobleman Tomaso Pecci, one of which, it seems, was not previously known (no. 46), are cataloged as three items (nos. 44–46). At the beginning of the seventeenth century, Pecci was one of the strongest advocates on behalf of the *seconda prattica*, the principles of which he applied in his *canzonettas* and madrigals. Also, one of the fundamental works of the early Baroque, the famous *Scherzi musicali* by Claudio Monteverdi of 1607, were a part of the Cathedral Chapter's collection (no. 50). In its foreword, Giulio Cesare Monteverdi elaborated in detail an affirmation of the *seconda prattica* previously announced by his brother Claudio in his fifth book of madrigals (1605).[33]

Cechini's opus 12 of 1617 (no. 47) consisting of precomposed materials, built from short, imitational procedures of elaborated motifs; *canzonettas* consisting of several couplets, written in homophonic syllable, are cataloged in this section as well.[34] Considering that this collection was dedicated to Bondumiero Lupo, then priest in Hvar, it was undoubtedly intended for Hvar's audience and performers.[35]

A' 4 Voci

The section *A' 4 Voci* lists four collections of secular music (Table 6.1, nos. 51–54). However, there are no data about two of them. Given the title *Novelli fiori del Visconti* (no. 51), it can be presumed that the author of this unknown collection (probably consisting mostly of madrigals), was an Italian composer and organist at the court of Antonio Medici, active in Florence in the first quarter of the seventeenth century, although the mentioned title is not found among his Florentine-style madrigals.[36] Also, this writer has not found a composer named Persone (Penone?), and hence no data about his book of four-part madrigals are cataloged in the inventory (no. 54).

There are two more books of madrigals listed here, both printed in 1613. One of them is a work of the little-known early Baroque *Maestro di cappella* from Treviso Giovanni Paolo Costa (no. 52), while the other is a posthumous edition of madrigals by the south Italian composer Pomponio Nenna (no. 53). Nenna's madrigals were particularly influenced by Carlo Gesualdo da Venosa's dissonant musical language, colored by progressive, abundant use of chromaticism and sudden variations of tempo and rhythm.[37]

A' più voci

There are listed under the rubric *A' più voci* 15 cataloged collections printed in the period 1590–1627 and intended for various vocal and vocal-instrumental groups (Table 6.1, nos. 55–69). This section consists of secular works, with the exception of Cecchini's collection of sacred madrigals *Canti spirituali* (1613) for one to three voices with instrumental accompaniment of *continuo* (no. 61), representing one of the early examples of sacred monody, even in European terms. Cecchini signed it as the *maestro di capella* of the Split Cathedral, and it contains sacred pieces composed "per cantare, et sonare nel Clavicembalo, Chitarrone ó Altro Istromento." The note below the title, "raccolta da Stefano Canonici," suggests that the compositions in the collection were collected from various composers' manuscripts. Apart from being connected to the spirituality of the Passion of Christ—except for a few dedicated to the Virgin Mary, also related to the Passion—these compositions share similar musical elements, some joint motifs and phrases, and precomposed form. Regarding the similarity of textual and musical contents, the compositions in this collection sound as if they represent in some parts an open and variable form of the early Baroque Italian *cantata da chiesa*.[38]

Three more collections of Cecchini's secular compositions are listed as part of this batch. They were intended for one- to two-part singing groups with instrumental accompaniment. Among them is the third book of madrigals, *Amorosi concetti*[39] (no. 64), the only extant exemplar, while the other two, *Amarosa guerra* (no. 55) and *Arie, madrigali & cantate* (no. 56), primarily consisting of madrigals, arias, and instrumental forms, such as sonatas, *baletti*, and *ritornelli*, remain known in name only.[40]

The collections belonging to earlier dating include *Selva di varia ricreatione* (no. 65) for 3 to 10 voices (1590) and Convito musicale (no. 66) for 3 to 8 singing parts (1597), in which almost all styles and forms of the time are represented: madrigals, *capriccios*, arias, *canzonettas*, serenades, *villotas*, *balli*, *bataglias*. Their author was Orazio Vecchi,[41] master of his time and well established in Venetian circles together with Andrea Gabrieli and Claudio Merulo, who was in the service of the d'Este family in Mantova. Merulo employed the widest spectrum of sacred and secular genres and was quite famous for the madrigal comedies he wrote in the late sixteenth century.

Thanks to an entry in the Cathedral Chapter's inventory, we learn that one of the earliest operas, *L'Euridice* (no. 63), composed by Giulio Caccini in 1600, reached Hvar. Caccini was the pioneer of Florentine monody and early Baroque dramatic musical forms. Because the theater in Hvar existed after 1612, one may assume that *L'Euridice* was staged there. However, such an assumption may need to remain vague since the Venetian Vincenti's edition of 1615, extremely popular and used for chamber performances and didactical purposes as an illustrative example of *stile rappresentativo*, was preserved at the Cathedral Chapter's archive.[42] Besides Caccini, this section includes titles of collections of two more representatives of the early Florentine monody, Antonio Brunelli (no. 59) and Domenico Melli (no. 60), in which various secular forms are employed: madrigals, *canzonettas*, arias, and *scherzi* with accompaniment by *chitarrone*, harpsichord, or some other instrument.

This category includes the listing of two collections of madrigals by Giovanni Priuli, *Musiche concertate . . . libro quarto* (no. 67) and *Delicie musicali* (no. 68), intended for chamber vocal groups with instrumental accompaniment. They were written after the composer moved to Vienna to work in the service of King Ferdinand II of Habsburg. Accompaniment of *basso continuo* is obligatory in both works, and in the latter the element of vocal and instrumental contrast becomes very prominent.[43] As a composer, Priuli experimented with the greatest variety of styles "from polychoral sacred pieces to conservative compositions in *stile antico*, from few-voiced motets and monodies to elaborate concertato style"—[44]many of which reached Hvar in more than six of his collections (four sacred ones in the *Spirituali* section and two secular ones in the *A'più voci* section).

Alessandro Grandi is represented by one collection in this group as one of the most important northern Italian composers of the early Baroque period, whose greatest contribution was reflected primarily in the development of the *concertato* style, as well as secular solo cantatas and arias. These forms were included in his collection *Arie, et cantade*, listed in the Cathedral Chapter's inventory (no. 69) and intended for singing ensembles from two to three voices and two violins.

Miscellaneous

The section *A'più voci* lists four items separated by a horizontal line that do not belong to any of the previous categories (Table 6.1, nos. 70–73). Among them there are tablatures (no. 70), arrangements of originally vocal compositions for Spanish guitar, written by the Italian composer and guitar player Pietro Milioni.[45] Although their entry does not follow the precise numerical order of collection or edition kept at the former Cathedral Chapter's archive, Milioni's tablatures testify to the presence of one of the most representative selections of early Baroque guitar music, which naturally implies the existence of an extremely early practice of guitar playing in Hvar during that period.

There is another entry in this section that is related to early instrumental music: *La Banchierina* (no. 73), written for four unspecified instruments and printed in 1596 as part of the collection *Canzoni alla francese a quattro voci per sonare*. This collection includes instrumental and vocal-instrumental compositions by Adriano Banchieri, a composer, organist, and theorist from Bologna. Since *La Banchierina* was listed as an individual composition, it is possible that it had been kept as a manuscript. In the course of his analysis of sonatas by Cecchini's op. 23 (1628), Marco Di Pasquale claimed that "[this] group of sonatas clearly derived some of its aspects from the old-fashioned *canzon francese*, probably as filtered through the improved models of Giovanni Gabrieli and his more conservative followers. But, as far as simplicity is concerned, they are paralleled only by some widely-circulated instrumental pieces by Adriano Banchieri."[46] Naturally, the existence of a copy of *La Banchierina* as listed in the Cathedral Chapter's inventory advances the hypothesis that Cecchini was familiar with the piece, thus suggesting similarity between Cecchini's and Banchieri's instrumental compositions.

Furthermore, Cecchini could have been familiar with Banchieri's theoretical works, judging from the entry in his singing manual, *Cantorino utile a novizzi . . . del canto fermo*, from 1622 (no. 72), intended for imparting music instruction to secular and religious clerics. Also, (cathedral) instrumentalists in Hvar had access to a manual for the performance of *basso continuo* (no. 71), written in 1628 by Galeazzo Sabbatini, a composer and theorist from Pesaro, who is represented in the Cathedral Chapter's inventory by a collection of madrigals in *concertato* style (see section *A'più voci*, no. 57).

Following this overview of the music inventory's sections, it is necessary to provide a summary of the basic characteristics of the Cathedral Chapter's music collection by providing Tables 6.2–6.5, in which the material from Table 6.1 is presented according to authors, date, and publishers of the first edition and musical genres.

In Table 6.2 40 different composers are cataloged in alphabetical order; authorship remains unconfirmed for only few works (Table 6.2, nos. 1, 11, 12, 15, 27, 39, 40). The largest number of entries relate to the works of the Hvar *Maestro di cappella* Tomaso Cecchini (20 entries), followed by Giovanni Priuli (6 entries) and Tomaso Pecci (3 entries), while seven composers are represented by two entries each: Alessandro Banchieri, Alessandro Grandi, Claudio Monteverdi, Damjan Nembri, Serafino Patta, Galeazzo Sabbatini, and Orazio Vecchi. Thirty composers in the inventory have one entry each. The place of employment is known for about one-third of the cataloged composers, the majority of whom spent their lives in northern Italy, while the rest were active in the territories of Florence (Table 6.2, nos. 6, 7, 8, 26, 39), southern Italy (no. 11, 24), or the Croatian coastal area (no. 9 and partly 32). They are a bit older or younger than Cecchini, as corroborated by the dates of the first editions of the collections cataloged in the inventory, which overlap with Cecchini's lifetime or residence in Hvar (see Table 6.3). The first editions of only seven collections were printed in the last third of the sixteenth century, while the others were published during the first four decades of the seventeenth century, mostly between 1610 and 1629, when the Venetian early Baroque music reached full peak. Although it cannot be confirmed with certainty which of the (re)editions was kept among the Cathedral Chapter's music repository, if data about their first editions are taken into consideration, it appears that most of them were printed in Venice, primarily for the Vincenti, while the publications printed in Bologna, Rome, Naples, and Florence are represented by one or two items (see Table 6.4).

Secular and sacred musical genres represented in the collections listed in the Cathedral Chapter's inventory are shown in Table 6.5.[47] It is interesting to note that most of the cataloged entries relates to secular (40 entries) and fewer to sacred music (31entries). Among the latter, the motet is the most represented genre (14 out of 16 entries), followed by settings of psalms (10 entries) and masses (eight entries). The remaining entries include responsories (Table 6.1, no. 24), spiritual madrigals (nos. 38, 40), *canzonettas* (nos. 30, 38), lamentations (no. 16), and instrumental *canzonas* and sonatas (nos. 5, 6).

Secular music accounts for a total of 40 entries, with collections consisting of primarily madrigals (23 out of 24 entries) in addition to arias (12 entries) and *canzonettas* (11 entries) and, to a lesser extent, *villanellas* (no. 43), *scherzi* (nos. 50, 59), cantatas (nos. 67, 69), and instrumental compositions (nos. 55, 56, 70, 73).

Compositions of church provenance found in the Cathedral Chapter's archive could have been heard in the Hvar Cathedral by all of the island's social classes, the music being mostly performed by the cathedral musicians conducted by Cecchini. But, since in the eighteenth century concerts, recitals, and various forms of entertainment were performed at the Bishop's Palace before an audience consisting of clergy and citizens,[48] the possibility that the same venue hosted (sacred) performances in the seventeenth century cannot be excluded.

Furthermore, a number of items related to the collections of secular music confirms that Tomaso Cecchini, definitely the most zealous beneficiary of the Cathedral Chapter's music archive, was engaged from time to time for secular performances, as were his predecessors, "in line with the old custom that the cathedral organist plays at the Duke's Palace during carnival time."[49] Therefore, it is probable that Cecchini conducted and participated in performances for the Duke and his guests at the Duke's Palace, using secular music works borrowed from the Cathedral Chapter's archive. However, with the establishment of the communal theater in 1612, Hvar got another space suitable for secular repertoire performances—in addition to the existing stage in the open town square—which could have been heard by citizens and visitors of Hvar, regardless of their social strata, a very progressive idea for the time.[50] Although there are no data about theater performances in the first decades after the theater's establishment during Cecchini's service in Hvar, one can presume that secular musical repertoire, such as that cataloged in the Cathedral Chapter's inventory, was also performed there, and the possibility of dramatic music performances, as suggested by the entry related to Caccini's early Baroque opera *L'Euridice*, cannot be neglected either.

Although some of the music collections listed in the Cathedral Chapter inventory are considered lost and the occasions and context of their performances in Hvar still remain unknown, they present an important source for further research into music in seventeenth-century Hvar. Also, they serve as indicators of musical practice in other Croatian coastal towns, where similar

(Italian) repertoire might have been nurtured as well, considering the strong cultural, economic, and/or political connections of this region with the other side of the Adriatic at that time. This music inventory corroborates not only the presence of contemporary Italian (mostly Venetian early baroque) music literature on the island of Hvar but also proves the existence of a systematic practice of collecting and cataloging printed music in Croatian church institutions prior to its being formally known and considered at the start of the eighteenth century. Additionally, the inventory may be helpful in better tracing Italian music historiography, since the nominal trace of music collections (some of them yet unknown), written by Italian composers, published by Italian publishing establishments, and distributed from Italy, once kept and cataloged as a part of the Cathedral Chapter Library, explicitly testifies to the dispersion and presence of Italian, mostly Venetian, early Baroque music literature on the eastern part of the Adriatic coast.

Tables

Table 6.1 Transcriptions of the titles listed in the Cathedral Chapter music inventory (Hvar, 1646/47)

Section	No.	Transcription of the title	Data about 1st edition (publisher, year, RISM)
A' cinq[ue] Voci [p. 18]	1	*Madrigali del Cecchino*	A. Vincenti, Venezia, 1619 [RISM A/I: C 1676]
	2	*Del Monteverde. Lib. 6.*	R. Amadino, Venezia, 1614 [RISM A/I: M 3490]
	3	*Del Riccio. Lib. 1.*	A. Gardano, Venezia, 1567 [RISM A/I: R 1294]
	4	*Del Barera. Lib. 2.*	
Spirituali [p. 20]	5	*Par. p.ª S Sacro[rum] Concentu[um] Io. Prioli*	B. Magni, Venezia, 1618 [RISM A/I: P 5476]
	6	*Pars 2.ª*	B. Magni, Venezia, 1619 [RISM A/I: P 5477]
	7	*Psalmi Eiusdem*	Venezia, 1621 (lost)
	8	*Missae Eiusdem*	B. Magni, Venezia, 1624 [RISM A/I: P 5478 ili RISM A/I: P 5479]
	9	*Missa c[um] Psālmis et. S. Cantionib[us] 1, 2, et 3. Vocib[us] D. Vincent. de Tutÿs à Grauina*	A. Vincenti, Venezia, 1628

(*Continued*)

Table 6.1 (Continued)

Section	No.	Transcription of the title	Data about 1st edition (publisher, year, RISM)
Spirituali—Cecchino [p. 20]	10	*Otto Messe à 4 voci pari sop.*ª *li otto Toni*	G. Vincenti, Venezia, 1617 [RISM A/I: C 1672]
	11	*3.º Libro delle Messe ariose à 3, 4, 5, et 8. Con salmi*	A. Vincenti, Venezia, 1624 [RISM A/I: C 440]
	12	*Messa, Salmi, et Motetti à 7 in due Chori*	G. Vincenti, Venezia, 1620
	13	*2º Libro de Motetti à 2*	G. Vincenti, Venezia, ?1613/4–1616/7? (lost)
	14	*Salmi e Motetti à 3. Lib. p.º.*	
	15	*Salmi e Motetti à 4. Lib. p.º.*	G. Vincenti, Venezia, 1616
	16	*Lamentationi à 2 col Miserere*	G. Vincenti, Venezia, ?1616/13–1616/17? (lost)
	17	*Psalmi, Missa, et alia cantica. 5 Vocib.*	A. Vincenti, Venezia, 1619 [RISM A/I: C 1675]
	18	*Cinque Messe à 2 Voci e Motetti à voce sola*	A. Vincenti, Venezia, 1628 [RISM A/I: C 1677]
	19	*P.º Libro de Motetti à 2*	R. Amadino, Venezia, 1613 [RISM A/I: C 1670]
	20	*3.ˢ Liber S. Concentu[um] 2 Vocib.*	
Spirituali [p. 20]	21	*Motetti à 1, 2, 3, et 4 raccolti dal Malgarini*	G. Vincenti, Venezia, 1618
	22	*Sacri Concentus F. Gabrielis de Pulitis 1, 2, 3 Vocib.*	G. Vincenti, Venezia, 1614 [RISM A/I: P 5652]
	23	*Salteri[um] D. Eustachio Arivieri à 2, 3, 4. Lib. p.º*	
	24	*Respon[sor]ia Hebdomada S. Gualterij 4 Vocib.*	
	25	*3.º Libro de i Concerti Ecc.*ᶜⁱ *del Porta à 2, 3, 4, e 5*	A. Vincenti, Venezia, 1619 (lost)

Section	No.	Transcription of the title	Data about 1st edition (publisher, year, RISM)
Spirituali [p. 20]	26	*Lib. 3.ˢ Sacro[rum] Cantico[rum] Patt[ae] 1, 2, 3, 4, 5, Vocib.*	
	27	*Lib. 4 de Motetti del Grandi à 2, 3, 4, 7*	G. Vincenti, Venezia, 1616 [RISM A/I: G 3431]
	28	*Psalmi Accademici Affectuosi 3 Vocib. et 4.*	
	29	*Psalmi D. Damiani Nembri. 4 Vocib.*	B. Magni, Venezia, 1641 [RISM A/I: N 377]
	30	*Canzonette Sp[iritu]ali del Zuchini à 3 lib. p.º*	
	31	*Missae Harmonicae Nembri. 3, 4, et 8 Vocib.*	B. Magni, Venezia, 1640 (lost)
	32	*Motetti à Voce sola del Cecchino*	G. Vincenti, Venezia, 1617 [RISM A/I: C 1674]
A' Voce sola [p. 20]	33	*Canzonette raccolte dal Stefani. p.º 2, 3, et 4*	*1st book*: G. Vincenti, Venezia, 1618 [RISM B/I: 1618–15]; *2nd book*: Vincenti?, Venezia?, 1619 (lost); *3rd book*: A. Vincenti, Venezia, 1623 [RISM B/I: 1623–10]; *4th book*: Venezia, 1626 (lost)
	34	*Arie del Miniscalchi. lib.1.*	A. Vincenti, Venezia, 1625 [RISM A/I: M 2851]
	35	*Arie del Pesenti.*	*1st book* (lost) and/or *2nd book*: A. Vincenti, Venezia, 1633 [RISM A/I: P 1545] and/or *3rd book*: A. Vincenti, Venezia, 1636 [RISM A/I: P 1547]
	36	*Arie del Berti. p.º et 2.º*	*1st book*: A. Vincenti, Venezia, 1624 [RISM A/I: B 2135]; *2nd book*: A. Vincenti, Venezia, 1627 [RISM A/I: B 2136]
	37	*Ariose Vaghezze del Milanuzij. 5.º et 6.º*	*5th book* (lost): p1624–1628; *6th book*: A. Vincenti, Venezia, 1628 [RISM A/I: M 2749]
	38	*Madrigali e Canzonette sp[iritu]ali del Bonini*	C. Marescotti, Firenze, 1607 [RISM A/I: B 3494]

(*Continued*)

Table 6.1 (Continued)

Section	No.	Transcription of the title	Data about 1st edition (publisher, year, RISM)
	39	*Amorosi Concetti del Cecchino, dopo i Scherzi de Mo[n]teverde. Lib. i.*	R. Amadino, Venezia, 1612 [RISM A/I: C 1668]
	40	*Motetti et Madrigali Sacri del Patta.*	B. Magni, Venezia, 1614 [RISM A/I: P 1039]
A' 2 Voci [p. 29]	41	*Madrigaletti del Cechini*	Venezia, 1623 (lost)
A' 3 Voci [p. 29]	42	*Canzonette di D. Marino Pesaro*	A. Raverii, Venezia, 1608 [RISM A/I: P 1499]
	43	*Vilanelle di Luca Marenzio*	*1st book*: G. Vincenti & R. Amadino, Venezia, 1584 [RISM A/I: M 587] and/or *2nd book*: [G. Vincenti, Venezia, 1592] [RISM A/I: M 596] and/or *3rd book*: A. Gardano, Roma, 1585 [RISM A/I: M 599] and/or *4th book*: G. Vincenti, Venezia, 1587 [RISM A/I: M 604], 1592 and/or *5th book*: G. Scotto, Venezia, 1587 [RISM A/I: M 608]
	44	*Canzonette dell'Affettuoso et inuaghito. P.º et 2º.*	G. Vincenti, Venezia, 1603 [RISM A/I: P 1109 i P 1113]
	45	*[Canzonette] Del Pecci. p.º*	G. Vincenti, Venezia, 1599 [RISM A/I: P 1102]
	46	*[Canzonette] Dell'Affetuoso. 4.º*	
A' 3 Voci [p. 29]	47	*Madrigali et Canzonette del Cecchino*	G. Vincenti, Venezia, 1617 [RISM A/I: C 1673]
	48	*Madrigali del Filibero. Lib. 1.*	
	49	*Baletti del Gastoldi*	R. Amadino, Venezia, 1594 [RISM A/I: G 534]
	50	*Scherzi Musicali à 3 del Monteverde*	R. Amadino, Venezia, 1607 [RISM A/I: M 3485]
A' 4 Voci [p. 29]	51	*Novelli fiori del Visconti*	
	52	*Madrigalli del Costa*	A. Gardano, Venezia, 1613 [RISM A/I: C 4223]
	53	*Madrigali del Nenna*	G. B. Gargano & L. Nucci, Napoli, 1613 [RISM A/I: N 398]
	54	*Madrigali del [Persone]*	

Section	No.	Transcription of the title	Data about 1st edition (publisher, year, RISM)
A' più voci [p. 41]	55	*Amorosa Guerra del Cecchino à 1 et 2*	A. Vincenti, Venezia, 1627 (lost)
	56	*Diversità da Canti del Cecchino à 1 et 2*	A. Vincenti, Venezia, 1630 (lost)
	57	*Madrigali del Sabbatini. Lib. 1. à 2, 3, et 4*	A. Vincenti, Venezia, 1625 [RISM A/I: S 11]
	58	*Concerti del Ferrari ò Madrigali. Lib. 1. à 2, 3, et 4*	
	59	*Arie, Scherzi del Brunelli. à 1, 2, e 3. P.º et 2.º*	*1st book*: G. Vincenti, Venezia, 1613 [RISM A/I: B 4645]; *2nd book*: G. Vincenti, Venezia, 1614 [RISM A/I: B 4646]
	60	*P.ᵉ et 2.ᵉ Musiche del Megli. à 1, et 2.*	*1st and 2nd book*: G. Vincenti, Venezia, 1602 [RISM A/I: M 1752 i M 1754]
	61	*Canti Spirituali del Cecchino. à 1, 2, e 3.*	G. Vincenti, Venezia, 1613 [RISM A/I: C 1669]
	62	*Quinto Libro della Canzonette del Radesca. à 1, 2, e 3.*	G. Vincenti, Venezia, 1617 [RISM A/I: R 22]
	63	*Euridice del Caccini.*	G. Marescotti, Firenze, 1600 [RISM A/I: C 4]
	64	*Amorosi concetti del Cecchino Lib. 3. à 1, e 2. dopo i Scherzi del Monteverde*	G. Vincenti, Venezia, 1616 [RISM A/I: C 1671]
	65	*Selva d'Horatio Vecchi*	A. Gardano, Venezia, 1590 [RISM A/I: V 1044]
	66	*Conuito dell'istesso*	A. Gardano, Venezia, 1597 [RISM A/I: V 1050]
	67	*Musiche concertate del Prioli Lib. 4.*	B. Magni, Venezia, 1622 [RISM A/I]
	68	*Delicie Musicali dell'istesso*	B. Magni, Venezia, 1625 [RISM A/I: P 5483]
	69	*Arie et cantada à 2 et 3. del Grandi*	A. Vincenti, Venezia, 1626 [RISM A/I: G 3473]

(*Continued*)

Table 6.1 (Continued)

Section	No.	Transcription of the title	Data about 1st edition (publisher, year, RISM)
Untitled section [p. 41]	70	*Intavolatura [per] la Chitarra del Millioni.*	G. Facciotti, Roma, 1627 [*1st-3rd book*: RISM A/I: M 2834 and/or *4th book*: M 2838 and/or *5th book*: 2840]
	71	*Regola [per] Sonare sop.ᵃ il Basso Continuo del Sabbatini*	Salvadori, Venezia, 1628 [RISM B/V, p. 742d]
	72	*Cantorino il Canto fermo del Banchieri.*	B. Cochi, Bologna, 1622 [RISM B/V, p. 113g]
	73	*La Banchierina del medesimo.*	R. Amadino, Venezia, 1596

Table 6.2 Authors of works listed in the Cathedral Chapter music inventory (Hvar, 1646/47)

No.	Author	Unit (see Tab. 1)	Total no. of units
1	ANONYMUS	No. 28	1
2	ARIVIERI, Eustachio	No. 23	1
3	BANCHIERI, Adriano (1568–1634)	Nos. 72, 73	2
4	BARERA, Rodiano (mid-16th ct.–1623)	No. 4	1
5	BERTI, Giovanni Pietro (c1600–1638)	No. 36	1
6	BONINI, Severo (1582–1663)	No. 38	1
7	BRUNELLI, Antonio (1577–1630)	No. 69	1
8	CACCINI, Giulio (1551–1618)	No. 63	1
9	CECCHINI, Tomaso (c1580–1644)	Nos. 1, 10, 11, 12, 13, 14, 15, 16, 17, 18, 19, 20, 32, 39, 41, 47, 55, 56, 61, 64	20
10	COSTA, Giovanni Paolo (act. 1610–1614)	No. 52	1
11	?FERRARO (FERRARI), Antonio? (act. 1613–23)	No. 58	1
12	?FILIBERO?	No. 48	1
13	GASTOLDI, Giovanni (c1554–1609)	No. 49	1
14	GRANDI, Alessandro (c1586–1630)	Nos. 27, 69	2

No.	Author	Unit (see Tab. 1)	Total no. of units
15	?GUALTIERI, Alessandro? (?–1655) or ?GUALTIERI, Antonio? (?–1649/1650)	No. 24	1
16	MALGARINI, Federico (ed.)	No. 21	1
17	MARENZIO, Luca (c1553–1599)	No. 43	1
18	MELLI, Domenico Maria akt. poč. 17. st.)	No. 60	1
19	MILANUZZI, Carlo (?–c1647)	No. 37	1
20	MILLIONI, Pietro (1st half of the 17th ct.)	No. 70	1
21	MINISCALCHI, Guglielmo (act. 1616–1630)	No. 34	1
22	MONTEVERDI, Claudio (1567–1634)	Nos. 2, 50	2
23	NEMBRI, Damjan (1584–1648/9)	Nos. 29, 31	2
24	NENNA, Pomponio (c1556–1608)	No. 53	1
25	PATTA, Serafino (act. 1606–1619)	Nos. 26, 40	2
26	PECCI, Tomaso (1576–1604)	Nos. 44, 45, 46	3
27	?PERSONE?	No. 54	1
28	PESARO, Marino	No. 42	1
29	PESENTI, Martino (c1600–c1648)	No. 35	1
30	PORTA, Ercole (1585–1630)	No. 25	1
31	PRIULI, Giovanni (c1575–1626)	Nos. 5, 6, 7, 8, 67, 68	6
32	PULITI, Gabriello (c1580–1642/3)	No. 22	1
33	RADESCA (di Foggia), Enrico Antonio (2nd half of the 16th ct.–1625)	No. 62	1
34	RICCIO, Teodoro (c1540-c1600)	No. 3	1
35	SABBATINI, Galeazzo (1597–1662)	Nos. 57, 71	2
36	STEFANI, Giovanni (ed.) (act. 1618–1626)	No. 33	1
37	TUZZI (DE TUTIIS), Vincenzo (1st half of the 17th ct.)	No. 9	1
38	VECCHI, Orazio (c1550–1605)	Nos. 65, 66	2
39	?VISCONTI, Domenico? (?–1626)	No. 51	1
40	?ZUCCHINI, Gregorio? (c1540/c1560–p1615)	No. 30	1

Table 6.3 Dates (first edition) of works in the Cathedral Chapter music inventory (Hvar, 1646/47)

Date	Unit (see Tab. 6.1)	Total no. of units
1560–1569	No. 3	1
1580–1589	No. 43	1
1590–1599	Nos. 45, 49, 65, 66, 73	5
1600–1609	Nos. 38, 42, 44, 50, 60, 63	6
1610–1619	Nos. 1, 2, 5, 6, 10, 13, 15, 16, 17, 19, 21, 22, 25, 27, 32, [33], 39, 40, 47, 52, 53, 59, 61, 62, 64	25
1620–1629	Nos. 7, 8, 9, 11, 12, 18, 34, 36, 37, 41, 55, 57, 67, 68, 69, [70], 71, 72	18
1630–1639	Nos. [35], 56	2
1640–1649	Nos. 29, 31	2
Unknown	Nos. 4, 14, 20, 23, 24, 26, 28, 30, 46, 48, 51, 54, 58	13

Table 6.4 Publishers (first edition) of works in the Cathedral Chapter music inventory (Hvar, 1646/47)

Publisher	Unit (see Tab. 1)	Total no. of units
AMADINO, Ricciardo (Venezia)	Nos. 2, 19, 39, 49, 50, 73	6
COCHI, Bartolomeo (Bologna)	No. 72	1
FACCIOTTI, Guglielmo (Roma)	No. 70	1
GARDANO, Angelo (Venezia)	Nos. 3, 52, 65, 66	4
GARGANO, Giovanni Battista & NUCCI, Lucretio (Napoli)	No. 53	1
MAGNI, Bartolomeo (Venezia)	Nos. 5, 6, 8, 29, 31, 40, 67, 68	8
MARESCOTTI, Cristofano (Firenze)	No. 38	1
MARESCOTTI, Giorgio (Firenze)	No. 63	1
RAVERII, Alessandro (Venezia)	No. 42	1
SALVADORI (Venezia)	No. 71	1
VINCENTI, Alessandro (Venezia)	Nos. 1, 9, 11, 17, 18, 25, 34, [35], 36, [37], 55, 56, 57, 69	14

Publisher	Unit (see Tab. 1)	Total no. of units
VINCENTI, Giacomo (Venezia)	Nos. 10, 12, 13, 15, 16, 21, 22, 27, 32, [33], 44, 45, 47, 59, 60, 61, 62, 64	18
VINCENTI, Giacomo & AMADINO, Ricciardo (Venezia)	No. [43]	1
Unknown	Nos. 4, 7, 14, 20, 23, 24, 26, 28, 30, 41, 46, 48, 51, 54, 58	15

Table 6.5 Music genres represented in works in the Cathedral Chapter music inventory (Hvar, 1646/47)

Genre		Unit (see Tab. 1)
Secular	Arias	Nos. 1, 34, 35, 36, 37, 55, 56, 59, 60, 62, 65, 69
	Canzonettas	Nos. 33, 42, 44, 45, 46, 47, 59, 60, 62, 65, 66
	Madrigals	Nos. 1, 2, 3, 4, 39, 41, 47, 48, 51?, 52, 53, 54, 55, 56, 57, 58, 59, 60, 62, 64, 65, 66, 67, 68
	Other	Nos. 41, 43, 49, 50, 55, 56, 59, 60, 63, 65, 66, 69, 70, 73
Sacred	Masses	Nos. 8, 9, 10, 11, 12, 17, 18, 31
	Motets	Nos. 5, 6, 12, 13, 14, 15, 18, 19, 20?, 21, 22, 25?, 27, 31, 32, 40
	Psalms	Nos. 7, 9, 11, 12, 14, 15, 17, 23, 28, 29
	Other	Nos. 5, 6, 16, 17, 24, 26?, 30, 38, 40, 61

Notes

1. See more about the period under the third Venetian rule in Hvar (1420–1797) in Grga Novak, *Hvar through the Centuries* (Zagreb: Izdavački zavod JAZU, 1972), 73–192, and in Kovačić Joško, "Development of the City and the Port of Hvar as a Military and Maritime Center," *Sources and Contributions for the History of Dalmatia* 25 (2012), 106–129.
2. See preliminary review of the musical inventory of the Cathedral Chapter in Maja Milošević, "The Inventory of Music Materials of the Cathedral Chapter in Hvar, 1646/1647," *Arti musices* 46/2 (2015), 277–307. See also more detailed insight into their particular sections in Maja Milošević, "What Kind of Music Repertoire Might Have Been Performed to the Audience in the Town of Hvar during the 1st Half of the 17th Century?" *Hvar City Theatre Days* 42/1 (2016), 190–227. A slightly revised version of the latter publication, originally written in the Croatian language, is presented in this essay.

3. Digital version of *RISM* (*Répertoire International des Sources Musicales*, serie A) can be browsed on the website https://opac.rism.info/ (accessed on 21 October 2016).

4. Since part of the recorded music collections was published in several editions, it is not possible to determine precisely which of them were formerly kept in the Cathedral Chapter Library in Hvar. See data about re-editions in Milošević, "The Inventory of Music Materials," 284–300 (Table 1).

5. See more about the family, life, and work of Damjan Nembri in Dragan Plamenac, "Damjan Nembri of Hvar (1584–c. 1648) and His Vesper Psalms," *Musica Antiqua Europae Orientalis* 6 (1982), 669–685.

6. Ennio Stipčević, "Foreword," in *Damjan Nembri: Brevis et facilis psalmorum quattuor vocibus modulatio (Venetiis, 1641)* [critical edition], edited by Ennio Stipčević (Zagreb: Muzički informativni centar Koncertne direkcije Zagreb, 2005), xv.

7. Plamenac, "Damjan Nembri of Hvar," 669. It seems that four-part masses were mistakenly excluded from the title published by Walther, since the full title of the lost Nembri collection was *Messe et Mottetti a 3, 4, e 8 con basso ripieni se piace* (Venice: B. Magni, 1640). Cf. Ennio Stipčević, *Tomaso Cecchini* (Zagreb: Muzički informativni centar Koncertne direkcije Zagreb, 2015), 44.

8. See an extensive bio-bibliographical study about Tomaso Cecchini in Dragan Plamenac, "Tomaso Cecchini, Chaplain of Cathedrals in Split and Hvar during the First Decades of the 17th Century: A Bio-Bibliographical Study," *Rad JAZU* 262 (1938), 77–125. See also Stipčević, *Tomaso Cecchini*, and his overview of Cecchini's life and work in the chapter "A Musician and His Society: Tomaso Cecchini in Split and Hvar," in Ennio Stipčević, *Ivan Lukačić and His Contemporaries* (Zagreb: Musica sacra, 1993), 47–73.

9. The pages on which musical sources were recorded do not follow each other immediately; perhaps the unbound sheets were scrambled at some point in time.

10. See Plamenac, "Tomaso Cecchini," 113, and Plamenac, "Corrections and Additions to the Bibliography of Works by Tomaso Cecchini," *Arti musices* 2 (1971), 48.

11. Walter Blankenburg and Norbert Dubowy, "Riccio, Teodoro," in *The New Grove Dictionary of Music and Musicians*, edited by Stanley Sadie (London: Macmillan, 2001) [hereinafter in endnotes: *NGroveD*[2]], vol. 21, 323.

12. Serena Dal Belin Peruffo, "Barera, Rodiano," in *NGroveD*[2], vol. 2, 724–725.

13. See Jerome Roche and Steven Saunders, "Priuli, Giovanni," in *NGroveD*[2], vol. 20, 384–385.

14. In that very same year (1624) Priuli published two collections of masses in Venice, the first one under the title *Missae . . . quatuor, sex, & octo vocibus concinendae, cum basso totius operis pro organo, si placet*, and the second one titled *Missae . . . octo, novemq. vocibus, atque etiam instrumentis musicis concinendae*. See data on both publications according to *RISM* number in Table 1, no. 8.

15. Plamenac, "Tomaso Cecchini," 95, 116–117. See the analysis of Cecchini's sonatas in Marco Di Pasquale, "Tomaso Cecchini's 'Sonate per gl'istrumenti, bassi, & soprani' from His Opus 23 (1628)," in *Zagreb and Music 1094–1994: Zagreb and Croatian Lands as a Bridge between Central-European and Mediterranean Musical Cultures*, edited by Stanislav Tuksar (Zagreb: Croatian Musicological Society, 1998), 105–125, and their critical edition: *Tomaso Cecchini: Eight Sonatas*, edited by Bojan Bujić (Zagreb: Muzički informativni centar Koncertne direkcije Zagreb—Muzikološki zavod Muzičke akademije Sveučilišta u Zagrebu, 1984).

16. See Di Pasquale, "Tomaso Cecchini's 'Sonate per gl'istrumenti, bassi, & soprani,'" 108–109. Two of Cecchini's lost collections that contained instrumental compositions were recorded in the Cathedral Chapter inventory as well (see Table 1, nos. 55 and 56).

17. See previous lists of Cecchini's works in Plamenac, "Tomaso Cecchini," 106–125; Plamenac, Corrections and Additions to the Bibliography of Works by Tomaso Cecchini," 43–52; Josip Andreis, *History of Music* (book 4) (Zagreb: Liber–Mladost, 1974), 87–89; Stanislav Tuksar, "Towards Identification of Four as Yet Unknown Later Works by Tomaso Cecchini from 1623, 1627, 1630 and 1634," *Arti musices* 24/1 (1993), 91–97. See recently revised list of Cecchini's works in Maja Milošević, "The Island of Hvar as the Meeting Point of Musicians in the 17th and 18th Centuries," in *Music Migration in the Early Modern Age: Markets, Patterns, Styles (2015)*, edited by Vjera Katalinić (Zagreb: Croatian Musicological Society, 2016), 115–116, and in Stipčević, *Tomaso Cecchini*, 100–120.

18. It may also be assumed that *Sacri concentus, liber tertius* was the third book in a series of works of sacred monody for two voices by Cecchini (see Table 1, nos. 13 and 19).

19. See more about Puliti and his music in Ennio Stipčević, "Introductory Observations on the Art of Gabriello Puliti (c. 1575–p. 1641)," *Arti musices* 14/1 (1983), 33–50.

20. Cf. Jerome Roche and Roark Miller, "Grandi, Alessandro," in *NGroveD²*, vol. 10, 283–287.

21. Composer Arivieri (Ariveri?) is mentioned only in Vincenti's catalog, as the author of motets for one- to four-singing parts (s. X, 13, and XXXII, 37, in Alessandro Vincenti, *Indice di tutte le opere di musica*, edited by Robert Eitner [Leipzig: T. Trautwein, 1882–1883], 8, 27), while there are no data about his life and work in the reference literature.

22. See Jerome Roche, "Gualtieri Alessandro," in *NGroveD²*, vol. 10, 472, and Jerome Roche and Elizabeth Roche, "Gualtieri, Antonio," in *NGroveD²*, vol. 10, 472–473.

23. See data about these editions according to *RISM* sign: A/I: P 1037 i P 1038. Cf. Gaetano Gaspari, *Catalogo della Biblioteca del Liceo Musicale di Bologna*, vol. 2 (Bologna: F. Parisini, 1892), 477, and Jerome Roche, "Patta, Serafino," in *NGroveD²*, vol. 19, 236.

24. See Wolfgang Witzemann, "Zucchini, Gregorio," in *NGroveD²*, vol. 27, 875.

25. See Maryann Bonino, "Bonini, Severo," in *NGroveD²*, vol. 3, 861–862.

26. The second book is considered lost. There is a third book mentioned in addition to the first one in the Cathedral Chapter inventory (no. 64).

27. See Nigel Fortune and Roark Miller, "Miniscalchi, Giuglielmo," in *NGroveD²*, vol. 16, 718.

28. See Roark Miller, "Berti, Giovanni Pietro," in *NGroveD²*, vol. 3, 458–459.

29. See Jerome Roche and Roark Miller, "Milanuzzi, Carlo," in *NGroveD²*, vol. 16, 672–673.

30. See Tuksar, "Towards Identification of Four as Yet Unknown Later Works by Tomaso Cecchini," 93.

31. See Steven Ledbetter and James Chater, "Marenzio, Luca," in *NGroveD²*, vol. 15, str. 835–845.

32. See Denis Arnold and Iain Fenlon, "Gastoldi, Giovanni," in *NGroveD²*, vol. 9, 567–568.

33. See Claude V. Palisca, *Baroque Music* (Croatian transl. by Stanislav Tuksar) (Zagreb: Hrvatsko muzikološko društvo, 2005), 15–19.
34. See more about Cecchini's op. 12 in Andrea Lengyel, "Tomaso Cecchini (Cecchino): Madrigali et Canzonette, Op. 12, Venezia 1617: A Contribution to the Development of Secular Music in Croatia in the 17th Century," *Arti musices* 14/2 (1983), 79–121.
35. See the content of inscription in Plamenac, "Tomaso Cecchini," 112.
36. See Nigel Fortune, "Visconti, Domenico," in *NGroveD*², vol. 26, 790.
37. See Keith A. Larson, "Nenna, Pomponio," in *NGroveD*², vol. 17, 752–753.
38. See Ennio Stipčević, *Croatian Musical Culture of the 17th Century* (Split: Književni krug, 1992), 84–85.
39. See the critical edition of Cecchini's op. 7: *Tomaso Cecchini: Amorosi concetti, il terzo libro de'madrigali a una, et due voci (Venetia, 1616)*, edited by Ennio Stipčević (Zagreb: Muzički informativni centar, 2006). This Cecchini opus is analyzed more elaborately in Bojan Bujić, "Cecchini's Third Book of Madrigals 'Amorosi concetti,'" *Musicological Annual* 2 (1966), 18–25, and in Iva Lovrec, "Poetic Models and Their Musical Settings: Tomaso Cecchini's 'Amorosi concetti' (1616)," *Arti musices* 24/1 (1993), 27–44.
40. See Tuksar, "Towards Identification of Four as Yet Unknown Later Works by Tomaso Cecchini," 93–94.
41. See Martin R. William, "Vecchi, Orazio," in *NGroveD*², vol. 26, 365–368. See more about Vecchi's works in Paul Schleuse, *The Singing Games in Early Modern Italy: The Music Books of Orazio Vecchi* (Bloomington: Indiana University Press, 2015).
42. See Metoda Kokole, "The Earliest Operas in Slovenia: From Euridice (?) to the Opening of the Estates Theatre in 1765," in *Centuries of Music in Slovenia* (Ljubljana: Festival Ljubljana, 2006), 230–231.
43. See Lawrence Bennett, *The Italian Cantata in Vienna: Entertainment in the Age of Absolutism* (Bloomington: Indiana University Press, 2013), 9–10.
44. Ibid.
45. With the exception of the fifth book, most of Milioni's intabulations were published before 1627, but these editions were not preserved. Therefore, the earliest known editions date from 1627 (see data about these collections according to *RISM* numbers in Table 1, no. 70). Cf. Gary R. Boye, "Milioni, Pietro," in *NGroveD*², vol. 16, 697–698.
46. Di Pasquale, *Tomaso Cecchini's* 'Sonate per gl'istrumenti, bassi, & soprani,'" 23, 115.
47. Two handbooks (see Table 1, nos. 71, 72) are excluded from Table 5.
48. See Stjepan Krasić, *Ivan Dominik Stratiko* (Split: Književni krug, 1991), 278–280.
49. Cvito Fisković, "Music, Theatrical and Other Events in Hvar in the 18th Century," *Hvar City Theatre Days* 5 (1978), 36.
50. See Mirjana Kolumbić Šćepanović, *Hvar and Its Theatre, 1612–2012* (Hvar: Grad Hvar–Muzej hvarske baštine, 2012), 25–28.

References

Bennett, Lawrence. *The Italian Cantata in Vienna: Entertainment in the Age of Absolutism.* Bloomington: Indiana University Press, 2013.
Kolumbić Šćepanović, Mirjana. *Hvar and Its Theatre, 1612–2012.* Hvar: Grad Hvar—Muzej hvarske baštine, 2012.

Krasić, Stjepan. *Ivan Dominik Stratiko*. Split: Književni krug, 1991.

Palisca, Claude V. *Baroque Music* (Croatian transl. by Stanislav Tuksar). Zagreb: Hrvatsko muzikološko društvo, 2005.

Schleuse, Paul. *The Singing Games in Early Modern Italy: The Music Books of Orazio Vecchi*. Bloomington: Indiana University Press, 2015.

Stipčević, Ennio. *Croatian Musical Culture of the 17th Century*. Split: Književni krug, 1992.

Stipčević, Ennio. *Ivan Lukačić and His Contemporaries*. Zagreb: Musica sacra, 1993.

Tuksar, Stanislav, ed. *Zagreb and Music 1094–1994: Zagreb and Croatian Lands as a Bridge between Central-European and Mediterranean Musical Cultures*. Zagreb: Croatian Musicological Society, 1998.

7   Migration of Musicians as an Integrative Principle

The Case of the East Adriatic Coast in the Eighteenth Century*

Vjera Katalinić

Introduction: A Case Study

Charles Burney sojourned in Venice for about two weeks in August 1770 as part of his Italian tour. There, he made the acquaintance of a certain Count Bujovich.[1] This noble envoy from the eastern coast of the Adriatic—the small town of Perast in the Bay of Kotor, then under Venetian administration—accompanied Burney to visit some places of interest that would have proven inaccessible to him without the intervention of an upper-class mediator. So, the distinguished Englishmen wrote: "he [Bujovich] had undertaken to get me some particular relative to the 1st establishment of music in the 4 conservatorj, which hitherto I could not get."[2] Burney also met with outstanding local musicians including Baldassare Galuppi, at that time *maestro di coro* at St. Mark Basilica, where the first organist was Ferdinando Bertoni, who, like Galuppi, taught at the *Ospedali*. Bertoni was known for maintaining a successful private studio. At this point, we see the development of a series of musical networks through which musicians from both sides of the Adriatic interacted. For instance, Bertoni's pupil Giovanni Battista Grazioli later entered service at St. Mark, and, most likely, Julije/Giulio Bajamonti, from Split, was a student of medicine at the University of Padua.[3]

Bajamonti and Grazioli remained in contact and exchanged letters with Antonio Bujovich, a cousin of the envoy from Perast. Burney gathered information on Venetian music life for his *General History of Music*; Bajamonti, on the other hand, traveled to Italy to study and consequently transplanted his knowledge of medicine as well as music to his native Split and other places where his work took him.

European Music Migration Research

Following the timelines of eighteenth-century musicians (performers and composers but also instrument makers, music teachers, writers on music, copyists, engravers, and printers), one may enlist patrons/Maecenas of music from both the professional and the amateur ranks as well as entire theater and opera companies, which were especially dynamic forces in the eighteenth century. This process unavoidably led to the creation of a network of itineraries that brought to fruition professional intersections and meeting points, a field of research explored by the EU project "Music Migrations in the Early Modern Age: The Meeting of the European East, West and South." This investigation included musicians' itineraries and acquisitions of musical material (sheet music and books on music) and musical instruments classified on a case-by-case basis. By the end of November 2016, six project groups from four countries (Germany, Poland, Slovenia, and Croatia) had collected data on 3,502 traveling musicians in the seventeenth and eighteenth centuries. The Croatian group alone gathered 520 entries complete with timelines and respective migration routes.

The Case of the Croatian Littoral

In the case of the Croatian lands during the long course of the eighteenth century up to the 1820s, some of the leading principles and main ideas arose from this methodological research, which, without major modification, could be applied to other geographical areas. Here, we focus on the eastern Adriatic coast down to the Albanian border by considering the following geographic areas:

1. The coastal area of Istria, the Croatian littoral islands, and Dalmatia, controlled by the Venetian administration until the fall of the Republic in 1797
2. The region of Dubrovnik, a semi-independent city-state that balanced politically between the West and the Ottoman Empire
3. A small portion of the coastal area of continental Croatia, whose main port, Rijeka/Fiume, experienced the influence of both central European and Mediterranean cultural and mobility issues.

In the turbulent history of musical culture in these areas—actually a sort of *Randgebiet* when viewed from Western (Roman Catholic) cultural centers bordering with the Ottoman Empire—the preserved primary and secondary sources of data on music are not numerous until the mid-eighteenth century. However, despite such unfavorable times for culture, some 200 names of migrant musicians connected with the Croatian littoral in the eighteenth century were entered in the project/common database.[4] These were musicians who participated in forming the mosaic of European music (both in Croatia and abroad) and its infrastructure. Their names were collected either from previous research results published in articles and books or directly from

primary sources. Annotated investigations about the itineraries and destinies of these musicians regarding their migratory issues were conducted.

Social Positions of Music Migrants

It can be stated that musicians belonging to all regions were migrating
individuals.

Nevertheless, musically educated members of the aristocracy usually
returned to their country of origin after the completion of their musical journey, as in the case of the father and son Luca and Antonio Sorgo, both noble-
men and composers. They returned to Dubrovnik after completing their
general and musical training in Rome. However, an exception can be found
in the personality of the mysterious violinist "Stephano N. detto Spadina,
gentiluomo Dalmatino" from Split, who was active at the court of the Polish
bishop Wojtiech Leski in Chelmno (Kulm) in the mid-eighteenth century. It
is possible that Spadina moved north after living in Padua for musical training. Although an aristocrat, Spadina was a professionally active composer
and chamber music player; therefore, he probably did not wish to reveal
publicly his full name. According to information furnished by publishers'
catalogs and some scant data preserved in Split and elsewhere, Spadina
never returned home.

Military musicians migrated quite frequently following their regiments.
Exceptionally, though, they left their military duties and settled as civilians,
usually as well-trained musicians. Only early nineteenth-century sources
kept more precise records of such cases, with emphasis on information
regarding Czech military musicians. For example, Johann Zayitz, a *Kapellmeister* in the "45th Baron Mayer Infanterie-Regimente," migrated to the
north Adriatic port of Rijeka in 1830, left the military, and settled as a civilian musician active in the local theater orchestra and as a private teacher.[5]
Already in the eighteenth century, central European military musicians were
musically better educated[6] than their colleagues in the Venetian military
corps stationed in Dalmatia, that is, *Fanti oltramarini* with their *piffari* and
suonatori di tamburo and *Cavalleria Croata* with *trombe da guerra* and
timpani.[7] Although the eighteenth-century documentation lists their names,
one can only assume that some of them, after leaving the army, joined some
local ensemble. However, proof of this has not yet been found, though the
documentation concerning the Croatian littoral has been compared with
entries in the database.[8]

Members of the clergy who dealt with music often migrated, following
their duties and orders. They usually did not leave the compounds of their
church or monastic community at large, so the firm bonds between church
communities on the Eastern and Western Adriatic coasts are easily traced.

Church musicians from the Italian areas entered church services in Croatia's coastal towns, where they stayed either temporarily or for life, depending on the availability of local musicians. Thus, Carlo Antonio Nagli, from Rimini, served for many years as *maestro di cappella* at the Cathedral of Split, but in 1743 he returned to Venice to assume similar duties at the Basilica dei Frari. The destiny of Bernardo Spinola was different, as he migrated from Venice to Split in 1724 to serve as a teacher and organist in the Franciscan monastery, joined the Cathedral in 1737, moved to Sibenik in the same year, migrated to the southern part of the Venetian Dalmatia, and died in Kotor.[9] Bernardo Pellizzari, from Vicenza, was retained as *maestro di cappella* at the Split Cathedral from the mid-eighteenth century to his death in 1789.[10] On the other hand, Jerolim Bernardi, from Split, sought musical education in Italy (Collegio Illyrico at Loretto) before returning to Split, where he served as the Cathedral organist.[11]

The larger of the groups under consideration is the one consisting of professional musicians who belonged to the lower social strata and who made their living from music making. This was the group that moved the most, according to the economic laws of supply and demand. For Italian musicians, the east Adriatic coast offered them various opportunities for making a living. Besides having church ensembles similar to those in Split and Zadar, Dubrovnik also supported the Rector's (Duke's) orchestra, where the Italian musicians Tommaso Resti, Angelo Frezza, Antonio Santoro, Antonio Bertolini, and Francesco Boriani, among others, were active. Although they often performed supplementary services in the Cathedral, their financial conditions were not prosperous mostly due to the parsimony of the Dubrovnik government. Therefore, they accepted some additional tasks such as private teaching (Frezza) or copying music material (Marino Santoro). Sometimes, the Dubrovnik government sent local musicians to Italian towns (mostly Naples) to receive training in the necessary music fields. A case in point was Vincenzo Klisevic, who was dispatched to Italy to learn how to play the double bass and to build and repair organs. At the end of the eighteenth century, the cities of Rijeka (from 1765)[12] and Zadar (from 1784)[13] welcomed Italian opera companies in their theatrical organizations, which became attractive centers for individual artists to teach and perform concert music. For instance, the violinist Angelo Maria Frezza emigrated to Dubrovnik from Italy in the 1780s for a short period of time, spent time teaching in Zadar, and then returned to Dubrovnik.[14] Giuseppe Michele Stratico, originally from Zadar, where he was born to a family of Greek immigrants, studied jurisprudence and music in Padua, remained in Italy, and died in Sanguinetto, near Verona in 1783.[15] Quite an extensive list of such migrants, most from Italy, was compiled for the Dubrovnik case. The Rector's (Duke's) orchestra, for instance, was in constant need of musicians.[16] The Republic of Dubrovnik handed over the task for searching for and attracting musicians and opera companies, as well as the acquisition of music material and musical instruments, mostly to their envoys in Italian towns, above all Naples and Rome.

Professional musicians were often regarded as artisans. However, secondary sources also identify some peasants who occasionally moved to towns in order to practice music or just to perform within their peasant group on special occasions, such as feasts of patron saints, and popular and attractive events.[17] Such cases were also entered in the project's database, but only when such individuals were known by name.[18] Short-distance migratory itineraries, hereafter defined as micro-migrations, were very important to the development of local communities.

Reasons for Music Migrations

The so-called push and pull factors defining migratory motives were numerous and usually combinatory: positive and negative or occasionally neutral connotations of some towns as well as secular and religious residencies within a region or cultural circle altered by political and economic changes, such as the abolition of the Venetian Republic in 1797, followed, in 1808, by the fall of the Dubrovnik Republic.[19]

Very often, the primary reason for the traveling was not musical but for other professional pursuits. For example, along with Luca and Antonio Sorgo, the Split composers Giulio Bajamonti and Antonio Alberti spent a few years in Padua to study medicine and jurisprudence, respectively. At the same time, they undoubtedly took music lessons and attended many musical events, and Bajamonti composed a few secular pieces in Padua and in nearby Venice.

The common desire to gain higher music education outside Croatian lands was caused by the fact that there were no higher institutions or prolific composers to offer advanced musical training. Consequently, Croatian towns suffered from a lack of educated musicians. The existing ensembles were generally glad to accept foreign professionals, as was the case for the Rector's orchestra in Dubrovnik or of the theater orchestra in Zadar. This meant that some foreign musicians, once installed, remained either for short-term residencies or permanently. It must be pointed out here that many musicians were recruited abroad by special request of the Dubrovnik Council, which charged a certain Espertis, the Council's envoy in Naples, to engage violinists who could also play cello and double bass.[20] This accounts for the oboist Michael Bianchi's arrival in Dubrovnik, where he joined the Rector's orchestra in 1757.

Often, the reason for migrating reflected economic issues. Musician sought adequate professional opportunities that could lead to prosperous careers, as was the case with Tomaso Resti, who emigrated from Lecce in Apulia to Dubrovnik. It appears, though, that Resti's earnings were not sufficient to support his family. He then resorted to copying music for and/or dedicating his compositions to prominent members of the local aristocracy in order to improve his financial condition.[21] Later, following the abolition of the Dubrovnik Republic, Resti moved to Zadar and Split. The violinist Angelo Maria Frezza from Rome, a colleague of Resti's, was also dissatisfied with his salary, and his continuous petitions for compensatory raises became well known.

Moreover, in the political sense, music migrations were triggered in times of both peace and war. Peacetime enabled more relaxed musical practices and secured the chances for migrant musicians to travel and explore new performing opportunities. Such was particularly the case for itinerant opera and theater companies, mostly from Venice and Ancona, which toured the eastern Adriatic coast throughout the eighteenth century. On the other hand, wartime forced some musicians to escape their hometowns. Such was the case of the seventeenth century's Cristoforo Ivanovich, who described directly or obliquely his definitive departure from his hometown, Budva, for Verona and Venice motivated by fear for his life caused by "constant Ottoman intrusions."[22] Some musicians left Dubrovnik after the abolition of the Republic in 1808. After the Napoleonic wars, the people of the entire Croatian littoral, Dalmatia, and Dubrovnik became subject of the Austrian Crown. Dubrovnik's status experienced a regression, while Zadar remained the capital of Dalmatia; thus, like Split it became an attractive migratory destination.

Regarding the activities of military musicians, the movements of their regiments compelled them to follow orders and migrate as well. At the beginning of the nineteenth century, Austrian officers, soon followed by Czechs, stationed themselves in Dalmatia and Dubrovnik.

Directions and Scopes of Migrations

At first, it should be stated that the term "migration," in its broadest sense, connotes movements of people whose intention is to stay in a new place for a long period of time or even permanently. Although it usually implies leaving for another country, migration within one's country or region is also important (micro-migration, as suggested earlier). In our project's database, we have registered both categories. An example of macro-migration in the stricter sense would be the early eighteenth-century peasant Francisco Glegh (Gled), an oboist in the Dubrovnik Rector's orchestra who arrived from a hinterland village to pursue music education.[23] A similar case occurred when the composer Giulio Bajamonti, from Split, moved to the neighboring island of Hvar, where he served for six years as a physician, cathedral organist, and composer in Hvar, the island's main town. However, it seems that distant migrations were more fruitful, connecting the hometown area with the new location, mostly in another country, but usually within the same cultural circle. Thus, the majority of musicians migrated between Italian towns and the east Adriatic coast (within either Venetia Dalmatia or the Republic of Dubrovnik). Yet, owing to Dubrovnik's specific status, musical contacts transcended that scheme, although primarily for nonmusical reasons (e.g., diplomacy, trade). One of the rare exceptions was the already mentioned Spadina, who traveled further north, either through Italy or by way of a more direct route, to reach his destination. The port of Rijeka was an exception concerning the issue of cultural circles. Although belonging to Ban's Croatia, and thus subjected to German and later Hungarian administrations, Rijeka was an Adriatic town exposed to Italian music and culture. Consequently, musicians flocked to this town from various directions, as evidenced by the origins of their names at the turn of the century: Francesco Purckardhoffer, Antonio Nava, Stefan Kordina, or Wenzel.[24]

Length of Sojourn at New Locations

As already pointed out, the issue of migration usually implied long sojourns in new environments. Lengths of visits varied between a couple of years and very long periods or even lifetimes. Usually, the length of stay depended upon the reason for migration. If a musician left for his education, he would return after a few years (an exception was Stratico, who stayed in Italy permanently). If the migrant musician wanted to establish himself professionally (as civilian or as a member of the clergy), he usually never returned home (Ivanovich). The destinies of military musicians need to be further investigated in order to draw more targeted conclusions.

Intersections/Meeting Points

Orchestras were preeminent meeting points for musicians, not only among themselves but among their hosts as well. Such was the case of Stratico's activity in Tartini's orchestra, where he learned contemporary performance practices and composition. On the other hand, schools and universities were meeting points for Croatian musicians who studied abroad in towns like Padua, Venice, Bologna, Rome, and Naples. These towns were influential because of their rich(er) and strong(er) musical infrastructures. They offered stylistic variety and good performance opportunities and gave impetus to changes in musical style, settings, and performance practices. Moreover, a certain hierarchy of musically important towns in Croatian lands can also be established. Although they were not "opinion makers" for questions of musical taste in general, they definitely attracted domestic and foreign musicians hoping to nurture their careers there. Dubrovnik was definitely at the top of the list, partly because of its relatively well-off citizens but also for its (relative) independence in terms of cultural policy. Rijeka, as a strong trade center, also offered adequate opportunities to active musicians, a situation obvious since 1765, when the first theater on the East Adriatic coast was built there. Split and Zadar followed as religious and administrative capitals.

Migratory Infrastructure (Networking)

Whenever data were preserved, it can be proved that targeted migration was prepared in advance and that strongholds to support such migration already existed to some extent. The network of relatives, diplomatic missions, friends of friends, former student mates, and related monasteries or colleges (such as San Girolamo in Rome or Collegium Illyricum in Loretto) was carefully built up for the benefit of the migrating musicians. Such networks also needed to be established in order to invite a good opera company (see, for instance, the Antonio Sorgo-Giulio Bajamonti correspondence), a reputed teacher, or a *maestro di cappella* from abroad (Dubrovnik's diplomats) or even for the purchase of instruments and music material. In that sense, the musical archives in Dubrovnik, rich with thousands of preserved sheets of music from the eighteenth century, testify that its aristocratic and educated bourgeoisie ordered music material from all major European printing establishments—in England, Germany, Austria, and Italy—in addition to using copyists' services at home and abroad. Thus, their repertoire was based mostly on imported musical works and tutorials in line with their individual taste and the inclinations of their musical practice.[25]

Music Impact

The benefits of migrants crossing both directions were especially significant in Croatian coastal towns: introducing new repertoire, promoting advanced performing practices and more sophisticated compositional skills and techniques that were implemented in the domestic communities. All this was, for the most part, welcomed. Sometimes, however, it elicited caution, especially with regard to innovations in church music (for example, there was a steady opposition to "figural" music within Franciscan communities) or when introducing opera companies in more traditional towns.[26] The relatively balanced dialogue and tension between tradition and innovation, wishes and possibilities, depended more on general economic and political situations than on artistic striving or employees' wishes.

Taking all this into account, it becomes obvious that musical culture on the eastern coast of the Adriatic during the century under consideration (and not only!) required more import than export. The lack of civic musical institutions intensified that need during peaceful periods, when music as representation, entertainment, or part of ecclesiastical services could develop more intensively. However, in that part of Europe, musicians—although still quite modest in their economic potential—usually did not have any problems with integration into new environments. The majority of those from the coastal area spoke Italian and were mostly Roman Catholic, and their nationality was not an issue at that time. According to the preserved documentation and to private statements (letters, diaries), they were well received on both sides of the Adriatic.

The situation in the nineteenth century brought some substantial changes. Newly established institutions brought to the fore issues of democratization; national strivings directed to some extent the musical/cultural political discourse (in the Croatian coastal area it happened a few decades later than in the continental area). For these reasons, the migration issue underwent transformations. However, some methods and research patterns used in the Music Migration (MusMig) project are applicable to models of music migration under these new conditions.

Notes

*   The topics discussed in this essay have been elaborated from the EU (HERA) project *Music Migrations in the Early Modern Age: The Meeting of the European East, West and South*, that concluded on 30 November 2016.
1.   Charles Burney, *Music, Men and Manners in France and Italy 1770*, edited by H. Edmund Poole (London: Eulenburg, 1974), 75.
2.   Ibid., 80.
3.   Bajamonti terminated his studies at the University in 1773 but continued quite regularly to visit Padua and Venice during the 1770s.
4.   See the MusMig database at its website: www.musmig.eu/database-test3.
5.   See "Migration and Cultural Transfer in Transformation: Czech Musicians in the 19th-Century Croatian Lands," in *Sociocultural Crossings and Borders: Musical Microhistories*, edited by Ruta Staneviciute and Rima Povilioniene (Vilnius: Lithuanian Academy of Music and Theater, 2015), 36–52: 49.
6.   The majority of military musicians at the end of the eighteenth century in continental Croatia and Slavonia (precisely in Karlovac and Osijek) made music also for private occasions and participated in the festive liturgy as church ensembles, as well as in theater orchestras (see Vjera Katalinić, "Emocionalno slavljenje pobjede: Prilog poznavanju glazbenih zbivanja u blizini proturske granice 1789" Godine [Emotional Celebration of Victory: A Contribution to the Knowledge on Musical Events in the Vicinity of the Border against the Turks in 1789], *Arti musices* 44/2 (2013), 187–200: 193).
7.   See Lovorka Coralic, Vjera Katalinić, and Maja Katusic, "Bubnjari, timpanisti, trubaci i pifaristi: Glazbena pratnja u mletackim prekojadranskim kopnenim

postrojbama u 18. Stoliecu" [Drummers, Timpanists, Trumpeters and Fifers: Musical Accompaniment in Venetian Overseas Army Units in the Eighteenth Century], *Arti musices* 47/1–2 (2016), 27–28.

8. Nevertheless, there might be some hints as to possible family connections: a young drummer, Giorgio Alberti, from Palmanova, joined the Dalmatian corps in 1727 in Venice (ibid., 44). He bears the same name as a seventeenth-century author of a tutorial titled *Dialogo per imparare con brevità à cantar canto figurato*; this Giorgio Alberti originated from the island of Hvar and published it in Venice in 1619. On the other hand, Antonio Alberti, a lawyer originating from Split and trained in Italy, was serving in his native town as *maestro di cappella* (1801–1804) after Giulio Bajamonti's death. Yet, the caution is necessary, because of the very common family name on both sides of the Adriatic. The same applies to Daniele and Santo Ivanovich, two late eighteenth-century drummers, and a *pifaro* Mattio Ivanovich (ibid., 57), who might have descended from the same family as the seventeenth-century theater historian Cristoforo Ivanovich, a Catholic canon at St. Mark in Venice and the author of the well-known *Minerva al tavolino* (Venice, 1681).

9. Nikola Mate Roscic, "Glazbena tradicjia samostana Sv. Frane na Obali u Splitu od 1600. Do 1900" [Musical Tradition of the Monastery of St. Francis at the Waterside in Split from 1600 to 1900], *Arti musices* 21/1 (1990), 5–44.

10. Miljenko Grgic, *Glazbena kultura u splitskoj katedrali 1750–1940* [Musical Culture in the Split Cathedral, 1750–1940] (Zagreb: HDM, 1997), 33–38.

11. Ivan Boskovic, "Nepoznati splitski orguljasi XVII I XVIII stoljeca" [Unknown Split Organists of the 17th and 18th Centuries], *Arti musices* 6 (1975), 85–98.

12. Rijeka lacks the documentation for its first purpose-built theater by the merchant Bono. More traces have been preserved about its second theater, the so-called Adamic Theater, from the very beginning of the nineteenth century.

13. The *Teatro Nobile* was organized as a joint venture by the local nobility.

14. Katica Buric, *Glazbeni zuvot Zadra u 18. i prvoj polovici 19. Stoljeca* [Musical Life of Zadar in the 18th and in the First Half of the 19th Century] (Zadar: Sveuceliste u Zadru, 2010), 33.

15. Lucija Konfic, "Josip Milhovil Stratico u Sanguinettu: Nova otkrica o skladateljevom zivotu i smrti" [Giuseppe Michele Stratico in Sanguinctto: New Discoveries about the Composer's Life and Death], *Arti musices* 43/1 (2012), 89–99.

16. Miho Demovic, "Glazba i glazbenici Dubrovackoj Republici od polovine XVII. do prvog desetljeca XIX. Stoljeca" [Music and Musicians in the Republic of Dubrovnik from Mid-17th to the First Decade of the 19th Century] (Zagreb: JAZU, 1989), 71–111.

17. The best-known were the feast of St. Blaise/San Biaggio, the patron saint of Dubrovnik, and St. Domnius/San Doimo, the patron of Split.

18. Most of the researched documentation originated from Dubrovnik: see Demovic, "Glazba i glazbenici Dubrovackoj Republici," 111–136.

19. On push and pull theory, see Everett S. Lee, "A Theory of Migration," *Demography* 3/1 (1966), 47–57: 49–52.

20. Demovic, "Glazba i glazbenici Dubrovackoj Republici," 100.

21. His name as copyist was inscribed on music material in possession of the aristocrats Jelena Pozza-Sorgo and Miho/Michele Sorgo. See Vjera Katalinić, *The Sorkocevices: Aristocratic Musicians from Dubrovnik* (Zagreb: MIC, 2014). Resti dedicated two arias, one to Miho Sorgo, the brother of the composer Luka Sorgo, and one to Antun/Antonio Sorgo, Luka's son. See Demovic, "Glazba i

glazbenici Dubrovackoj Republici," 229. For illustrations of Resti and Frezza's dedications see Katalinić, *The Sorkocevices*.
22. Stanislav Tuksar and Christoph Ivanovich, "A Seventeenth-Century Dalmatian Migrant in Serenissima," Revisited in *Music Migrations in the Early Modern Age: People, Markets, Patterns and Styles*, edited by Vjera Katalinić (Zagreb: HMD, 2016), 49–63: 52, 59.
23. Demovic, "Glazba i glazbenici Dubrovackoj Republici," 87.
24. Lavorka Ruck, "Glazbeni zivoit Rijeke" [Musical Life of Rijeka], in *Temelji modern Rijeke 1780–1830* [The Fundaments of the Modern Rijeka, 1780–1830], edited by Ervin Dubrovic (Rijeka: Muzej grada Rijeke, 2005), 153–168 (Catalogue of the Exhibition).
25. The example of the noble Gozze/Gucetic family from Dubrovnik has been analyzed in Vjera Katalinić, "Imported Music Scores in the Possession of the Gozze Family in Dubrovnik," *De musica disserenda* 9/1–2 (2015), 197–209.
26. The famous physicist Rogier Boscovich claimed in a letter in 1748 that introducing theater companies with female singers and actors would influence moral corruption of the citizens of the Republic of Dubrovnik (see Katalinić, *The Sorkocevices*, 18, according to Nada Beretic, "Iz povijesti kazalisne i glazbene umjetnosti u Dubrovniku" [From the History of Theater and Music in Dubrovnik], *Anali historijskog instituta Dubrovnik* 6/7 [1959], 329–357).

References

Buric, Katica. *Glazbeni zuvot Zadra u 18. i prvoj polovici 19. Stoljeca* [Musical Life of Zadar in the 18th and in the First Half of the 19th Century]. Zadar: Sveuceliste u Zadru, 2010.
Burney, Charles. *Music, Men and Manners in France and Italy 1770*, H. Edmund Poole (ed.). London: Eulenburg, 1974.
Demovic, Miho. *Glazba i glazbenici Dubrovackoj Republici od polovine XVII. do prvog desetljeca XIX. Stoljeca* [Music and Musicians in the Republic of Dubrovnik from Mid-17th to the First Decade of the 19th Century]. Zagreb: JAZU, 1989.
Dubrovic, Ervin, ed. *Temelji modern Rijeke 1780–1830* [The Fundaments of the Modern Rijeka, 1780–1830]. Rijerka: Muzej grada Rijeke, 2005 (Catalogue of the Exhibition).
Grgic, Miljenko. *Glazbena kultura u splitskoj katedrali 1750–1940* [Musical Culture in the Split Cathedral, 1750–1940]. Zagreb: HDM, 1997.
Katalinić, Vjera. *The Sorkocevices: Aristocratic Musicians from Dubrovnik*. Zagreb: MIC, 2014.
Katalinić, Vjera, ed. *Music Migrations in the Early Modern Age: People, Markets, Patterns and Styles*. Zagreb: HMD, 2016.
Staneviciute, Ruta and Rima Povilioniene, eds. *Sociocultural Crossings and Borders: Musical Microhistories*. Vilnius: Lithuanian Academy of Music and Theatre, 2015.

About the Contributors

Dinko Fabris obtained his PhD in Musicology from the University of London and the Diploma of Western Lute and Early Music from the Conservatorio di Music "E. F. dall'Abaco" of Verona. He teaches music history at the Conservatorio di Musica San Pietro a Majella in Naples and, since 2001, lectures at the Università degli Studi della Basilicata in Matera. He serves on the scientific boards of the international journals *Early Music*, *Cuadernos de Música Iberoamericana*, *Revista de Musicología*, *Lute Society of America Journal*, *Ad Parnassum*, and Musica *Disciplina* and on the scientific boards of the critical editions of the works by Andrea Gabrieli, Francesco Cavalli, and Jacomo Gorzanis. Furthermore, Fabris is co-editor of the New Edition of the works of Carlo Gesualdo. External professor in the doctoral program at the University of Leiden and Honorary Principal Fellow at the University of Melbourne, he serves as a member of the Academia Europaea and as music consultant to the Pontifical Council for Culture. Member of the Commission Mixte of RILM (2009–2016) and RISM (2017–2020), he was president of the International Musicological Society (2012–2017) and currently "last president" (2017–2022) and chair of IMS Regional Associations and Study Groups, including the newly created IMS Study Group on "Mediterranean Studies". Fabris's 150 publications include *Music in Seventeenth-Century Naples* (Ashgate 2007; reprint, Routledge 2016), *Partenope e il mito musicale di Napoli* (Cafagna 2016) and the critical edition of Cavalli's *Didone* (Bärenreiter, in preparation).

Francesco Zimei is a musicologist with an interdisciplinary training. His research has significantly contributed to the knowledge of important repertoires from the Middle Ages to the Baroque, mainly focusing on Italian *lauda*, *Ars nova*, late baroque *opera*, and the orchestral output of Johann Sebastian Bach. Most of these activities have resulted in the publication of several books and peer-reviewed articles and essays. As a strong advocate of the need for a close relationship between musicology and performance practice, he often interacts with renowned soloists and ensembles of early music. Founder and past chairman of the Istituto Abruzzese di Storia Musicale (www.iasm.it), he is currently the editor in chief of two scholarly series published by Libreria Musicale Italiana.

Franco Sciannameo, born in Apulia, Italy, is a violinist, musicologist, and cultural historian. He graduated from the Conservatorio di Musica "Santa Cecilia" in Rome and pursued further studies at the Accademia Chigiana in Siena, Accademia di Santa Cecilia in Rome, the University of Hartford, and the University of Pittsburgh. Always concerned with the role of artists in society, Sciannameo writes and lectures extensively on contemporary music and its relation to politics, cinema, and the arts. He has worked with a number of celebrated composers, including Giacinto Scelsi, Nino Rota, and Ennio Morricone, with whom he collaborated on performances and recordings. Sciannameo's articles and essays are featured in *The Musical Times* (London), and his most recent books include *Nino Rota's The Godfather Trilogy* (Rowman & Littlefield, 2010); *Phil Trajetta (1777–1854), Patriot, Musician, Immigrant* (CMS Monographs and Bibliographies in American Music, 2010); *Music as Dream: Essays on Giacinto Scelsi* [with Alessandra Carlotta Pellegrini] (Rowman & Littlefield, 2013); *Experiencing the Violin Concerto: A Listener's Companion* (Rowman & Littlefield, 2016), and *Ennio Morricone's Walk of Fame: From Darmstadt to Hollywood* (Lexington Books, forthcoming). Sciannameo is College Distinguished Teaching Professor of Applied Musicology in the College of Fine Arts at Carnegie Mellon University in Pittsburgh and visiting professor of applied musicology in the Faculty of Arts, Humanities, and Cultures at the University of Leeds, United Kingdom.

Jakša Primorac is a researcher in the Department of Ethnology at the Croatian Academy of Sciences and Arts in Zagreb. Since 2000, he has published a number of works in ethnomusicology, history, and ethnology. His primary research interest is multidisciplinary and includes comparative studies of music cultures in the Balkans and the Mediterranean. His recent research focuses on traditional singing in the coastal parts of Croatia and Montenegro, as well as in Italy (Quattro Province) and Greece (Ionian Islands). In 2013, Jakša Primorac published *Poj ljuveni*, a book on folk singing in Renaissance Dalmatia, and in 2015, together with Zlata Marjanović, he wrote *Pjesme dalmatske iz Boke Ludvika Kube (1907. g.)*, a book about Ludvik Kuba's note songbook from the Bay of Kotor. In recent years, Jakša Primorac coedited two books that analyze important ethnographic and partially musical material from the end of the nineteenth and the beginning of the twentieth century. The first book, *Toliški kraj*, published in 2014, deals with the area of Tolisa in the Bosanska Posavina region, while the second, *Luka Lukić: Učitelj, etnograf i melograf u Klakaru*, from 2016, focuses on the work of the Croatian ethnographer and melographer Luka Lukić, from the area of Slavonski Brod. In 2017, Jakša Primorac was an editor of Đorđe Begu's book about lyra-type instrument (*lijerica*) from the area of Dubrovnik. Currently, he is researching various styles of traditional polyphony in Croatia, the country that represents a specific crossroads of traditional multipart singing. This paper, which is to be published in 2018, discusses the origins and historical ties of certain polyphonic and monodic vocal styles.

Kostas Kardamis is a musicologist currently serving as Assistant Professor in the Music Department at the Ionian University (Corfu). He has collaborated with the Oxford University Press, the Megaron Athens Concert Hall, the Greek Composers Union, the Cultural Foundation of the Piraeus Bank Group, and the Durrell School of Corfu. His published studies, papers, and articles mainly concern Neohellenic music, with particular focus on the eighteenth and nineteenth centuries, as well as opera and musical theater. His research interests also include band music and the interaction of music, society, and politics. He is a member of the Hellenic Music Research Lab, the Greek committee for RILM, and the editorial committees of the musicological journals *Moussikos Loghos* and *Moussikos Ellenomnemon*. He is also the general editor of the series "Monuments of Neohellenic Music." Since 2003, he has been the curator of the Archive and the Museum of the Corfu Philharmonic Society.

Maja Milošević has been an assistant at the University of Split, Arts Academy, Department for Music Education, since 2011, teaching courses in musicology and ethnomusicology. She earned her MA degree at the University of Zagreb, Department of Musicology of the Academy of Music. Milošević is completing her PhD at the University of Zagreb, Faculty of Humanities and Social Sciences, with a thesis titled "Art Music on the Island of Hvar in Period from the 17th Until the First Decades of the 20th Century: Archival Music Collections in Hvar and Stari Grad," supervised by Dr. Sc. Vjera Katalinić. In 2015 and 2016, she was employed as junior researcher at the Croatian Academy of Sciences and Arts, Department for History of Croatian Music, in Zagreb, taking part in the international musicological HERA project "Music Migration in the Early Modern Age: The Meeting of the European East, West and South" (led by Dr. Sc. Vjera Katalinić). Currently she is participating as a researcher at the University of Split, Arts Academy, in the musicological project "Musical Sources of Dalmatia in the Context of the Central-European and Mediterranean

Musical Culture from the 18th to the 20th Century" (led by Dr. Sc. Ivana Tomić Ferić), financed by Croatian Science Foundation. Her main areas of research are historical musicology, music history of the island of Hvar, and musical archives and collections in Dalmatia.

Vjera Katalinić, scientific adviser and director at the Department for the History of Croatian Music, Croatian Academy of Sciences and Arts, in Zagreb, is a full professor at the University of Zagreb, Music Academy. Her fields of interest are eighteenth- and nineteenth-century musical culture, musical collections, and archives. Leader of the HERA project "Music Migrations in the Early Modern Age: the Meeting of the European East, West and South" (2013–2016), she has authored four books and more than 200 articles and is editor of 10 proceedings and six music scores. Her most recent book is *The Sorkočevićes: Aristocratic Musicians from Dubrovnik* (2014). She also serves as editor in chief of the journal *Arti musices*.

Index

For Product Safety Concerns and Information please contact our EU representative GPSR@taylorandfrancis.com Taylor & Francis Verlag GmbH, Kaufingerstraße 24, 80331 München, Germany

Printed and bound by CPI Group (UK) Ltd, Croydon, CR0 4YY
11/04/2025
01843992-0007